Spirit Tailings

*Men fear death as children fear to go in the dark;
and as that natural fear in children is increased with tales,
so is the other.*

Francis Bacon

Spirit Tailings

Ghost Tales of Virginia City, Butte, and Helena

By Ellen Baumler
With a preface by Jon Axline

Montana Historical Society Press

Cover Image: Forestvale Cemetery in Helena taken by Geoffrey Wyatt

Back Cover Image: *Montana Post* print shop window in Virginia City taken
    by Ellen Baumler

Cover Design: Geoffrey Wyatt

Book Design: Geoffrey Wyatt

Typeset in Adobe Caslon

Printed in Canada

Copyright © 2002 by Montana Historical Society Press, P. O. Box 201201,
Helena, Montana 59620-1201. All rights reserved

02 03 04 05 06 07 08 09 10 10 9 8 7 6 5 4 3 2 1

ISBN 0-917298-91-8

Library of Congress Cataloging-in-Publication Data

Baumler, Ellen.
 Spirit tailings : ghost tales of Virginia City, Butte, and Helena /
Ellen Baumler.
  p. cm.
Includes bibliographical references.
 ISBN 0-917298-91-8 (alk. paper)
 1. Ghosts--Montana. 2. Haunted places--Montana. I. Title.
 BF1472.U6 B38 2002
 133.1'09786--dc21
            2002003741

Table of Contents

List of Illustrations

Preface

SEVERAL YEARS AGO, ELLEN BAUMLER and I hiked a segment of the old road that once connected Bozeman and Virginia City, Montana. Formerly one of the most heavily traveled routes in pre-twentieth-century Montana, it is now mostly abandoned. Over it passed the lifeblood of Alder Gulch and Virginia City in the form of agricultural goods from the Gallatin Valley and, even more importantly, emigrants seeking their fortunes in the gold camps that lined the gulch.

One branch of this route included a toll road built by Joseph Albert Slade in 1863. Slade, a notorious hell-raiser, soon ran afoul of the local Vigilantes, who held a sham trial and then executed him as quickly as possible before his wife Virginia could interfere. Virginia had somehow gotten word of the pending lynching but couldn't make it in time. Locals say that her ghost still races her horse down the road in a futile attempt to rescue her doomed husband. The road brought an unknown number of people to the mining camp—the spirits of some, according to this book, are still there.

It is no wonder that the wild Montana mining camps have generated more than their fair share of ghost stories. The very names of Virginia City, Butte, and Last Chance Gulch conjure up images of wide-open towns where anything went. The camps were cosmopolitan urban centers, drawing in men and women of all nationalities, characters, and economic pursuits—some legitimate, some not—with varying notions of morality and decorum. For many, the camps were sources of opportunity and excitement; others encountered tragedy and violent death. Mining-town life was frenetic in its intensity with a "Let 'er Rip" attitude that left an indelible mark on the state's history. The vigorous tenor of life in the mining camps has made them ideal breeding grounds for many of Montana's best ghost stories.

Believers in ghosts suggest that hauntings are based on strong emotions and people's attachments to a particular place and era. For Virginia City, the energy of its denizens lasted only as long as the gold, but shades of people long-dead may still walk the boardwalks and inhabit some of its buildings. The buildings, "ghosts" of another kind, comprise Montana's best preserved gold rush community. Besides the midnight rides of Virginia Slade, its familiar spirits include at least one suicide victim, a nun, and a little girl.

In contrast to quaint, forgotten Virginia City, Butte developed an international reputation. Butte has come to epitomize the "Wide Open Town," infamous for its underground mines, hard drinking, brawling, and red-light district. The World's Greatest Mining Camp is also host to a remarkable set of ghost stories that contribute to the city's infamous reputation. But beyond the rambunctious nightlife, Butte has also known deep tragedy as evidenced by the 1917 fire in the Speculator Mine that took the lives of 168 miners whose deaths offer a haunting reminder of mining's unspoken dangers.

Like Butte and Virginia City, Helena originated as a mining camp with much of the same colorful character. It saw more than its fair share of hard and fast living and heartbreak. By the 1890s, though, politics had replaced gold as the city's lifeblood—in 1894's deeply corrupt election, Helena defeated Anaconda to become the permanent home of the state capital, a site that has often generated the same intense emotions and passions found in the other mining cities. As a long-time Helena resident with roots that go back to the late 1860s, I am acquainted with many of the historical figures populating Ellen Baumler's stories. Indeed, one tale has come to be associated with my recent family history.

In October 2000, my daughter Kate and I attended one of Ellen's annual Halloween readings at the Grandstreet Theatre in Helena. Although Kate and I disagree on lots of things, we share an interest in ghost stories. She has even been gathering them from her family and friends in an effort, she says, to help Ellen. At the program, Ellen recounted the story of Clara and the stained glass window reported in "The Lady of the House." Although I had heard the story many times while growing up in Helena, it never ceased to fascinate me every time I visited the building (especially when it was the city library). Kate, however, became terrified as the story unfolded and spent most of the evening looking around, afraid of seeing Clara looking back at her from somewhere in the building. Because of Ellen's oratorical ability and the effect it had on my daughter, the tale of the Grandstreet Theatre ghost has become a welcome part of our family history.

Although not completely convinced of the existence of ghosts (mainly because I've never actually seen one), I do believe that past events may have left some residual imprint on a place. That "spirit" could manifest itself as a feeling, a disembodied voice, or an apparition. Stories about the Quartz Street Fire Station, the section of the Bozeman Road above Virginia City, the Grandstreet Theatre, and others collected here are about the spirit and meaning of place. Some tales included here are amusing, others downright chilling, and all are lively in recounting the life and times of Montana's legendary mining towns. Pleasant dreams!

Jon Axline, 2002

Acknowledgments

I AM INDEBTED TO THE MANY GENEROUS, enthusiastic folks who graciously and honestly shared their experiences with me and allowed me to include them here. Their encounters added greater dimension to the history that ties these stories together; in many instances there would be no story without their personal accounts. I owe thanks to Grandstreet Theatre, the Helena *Independent Record*, Ellen Crain at the Butte-Silver Bow County Archives, Jill Verdon and Stacey Gordon, the Montana Heritage Commission staff at Virginia City, the Montana Historical Society, and in particular MHS Director of Publications Clark Whitehorn. Clark's belief in this project never wavered, and his skillful editing is evident throughout. I am especially grateful to my husband, Mark, and my daughter, Katie, for listening endlessly to my stories and then reading, rereading, and critiquing them.

Ellen Baumler
Helena, Montana
March, 2002

Introduction

ON A RECENT TRIP TO NEW ORLEANS I struck up a conversation
with a local tour guide. She was a native of the Louisiana bayous,
a region rooted in tradition and especially famous for folk legends
and stories of the supernatural. As is my wont when I travel, I
asked her about ghosts. She told me that there had always been
ghosts in her family; they were as familiar as her mother's china,
her father's fiddle, or her granny's wedding quilt. While most
people would have recoiled at the idea of ghosts in the attic, she
came to appreciate this family oddity and to count herself among
the lucky few for having grown up with ghosts. And she would
no more have doubted their existence than she would have sold
her family treasures. When it comes to ghosts, proof is a personal
thing. You won't find certainty that ghosts are real unless you
experience them first hand as did this lady from Louisiana. Even
then, doubts linger.

There is no proof here, but these Montana tales and legends offer an interpretation of the past as haunting as a Louisiana
bayou in the moonlight. For more than a decade I have been col-
lecting accounts of ghosts and eerie bits of this and that. Working with National Register properties and heritage places across
the state as a historian with the Montana Historical Society has
afforded me unique opportunities to research little-known stories
that Montana's places have to tell. Many people have generously
and honestly shared their experiences. I have checked facts and
matched them with the tools that are the stock and trade of the
historian: census reports, deed records, city directories, obituar-
ies, historic maps, and the like. Many of these tales have yielded
uncanny discoveries while others defy substantiation. The collection is organized around the historic mining camps of Virginia
City, Butte, and Helena. All three towns, as you will discover, have

generated their share of uneasy secrets, scary places and unsolved mysteries—*spirit tailings*.

My experience in my house in Helena piqued my curiosity about places that attract surreptitious visitors. My archaeologist husband Mark, daughter Katie, and I moved to Helena, Montana, in 1988 from Tucson, Arizona. We bought our historic home just in time to celebrate its 100th birthday, and we have since delved deeply into its history. We are acquainted with the two elderly grandchildren of a former owner. The brother and sister—now in their nineties—grew up in our house as did their mother; they have visited us and shared wonderful stories and memories about their beloved family home. And my family has its own stories about the house.

When my daughter Katie was little, before we knew much about the history of the house, she began to insist that it was haunted. I used to tell her that the house was old and its boards and beams creaked with age, not ghosts. But as her stories grew more specific, I began to wonder. John Wick, a well-known Helena saloon keeper, bought the house in 1898. He and his wife, Mina, were German immigrants who came to Helena on the heels of the gold rush. Wick, a carriage maker, lost his business to fire in 1884, then switched his career to saloon keeping. He died in 1908 and, as was customary, the wake was held in the house.

From the time she was about four, Katie began to insist that she heard "John" coming home from the saloon late in the night, his heavy tread on the stairs waking her up. She never seemed frightened of the footsteps, but she was terrified of the window in her room at the top of the stairs. She spent sleepless nights in dread of an unnamed terror peering in at her from the window as soon as she closed her eyes. In our own sleepless desperation we finally moved her to a different bedroom.

We had lived in the house several years when one day a previous owner knocked on the door and asked for a tour to see if the house was as she remembered. When we got to the room at the top of the stairs, she told me that the room had been her daughter's. She looked at me in a strange kind of way and said, "You know, as long as we lived here she could never sleep in this room. She was always afraid, and it had something to do with the window."

A few years later, an acquaintance who claimed psychic abilities asked for a tour. She knew nothing of our house at all, but when she stepped over the threshold into the room at the top of the stairs, she startled me with a loud gasp and clutched her chest, saying that the air felt heavy and she couldn't breathe. She had the same reaction in the downstairs den, directly below this bedroom.

Some time later during one of his visits, John Wick's ninety-three-year-old grandson told us about one of his few unpleasant childhood memories. He vividly recalled his mother's unreasonable fear of thunderstorms. She would take him into the closet in her bedroom, which is now our den, and shut the door. They would huddle there in the pitch black until the storm passed. He said he always felt that he would suffocate in the clothing in the dark closet. His intense feelings obviously left an indelible imprint.

Katie and I—and even Mark, the resident skeptic—have all had our sleep disrupted by a non-existent radio playing in the night. This began when we first moved in, and it has continued off and on to the present day. Sometimes we hear music, sometimes talking, sometimes only static, but it's always just low enough that you can't identify words or songs. This annoying nighttime disturbance almost always occurs during times of stress or illness. Each family member has heard it, and occasionally, we have all heard it at the same time. We learned from the grandson that in the 1910s and early 1920s he had Helena's first ham radio, which he kept in the room at the top of the stairs.

We have also awakened in the middle of the night to the smells of coffee brewing and bacon frying, and at holiday time, turkey roasting. Our two dogs bark at something in the kitchen, typically at about 9:45, six nights out of ten. Other incidents such as objects falling off shelves, tapping sounds, items disappearing, and electrical problems have contributed to our suspicions about the house. One night my cocker spaniel—who was deaf as a post—was lying on the bathroom floor while I took a shower. A picture suddenly flew off the wall. It didn't *fall*; it hit a foot from the wall, landing on the floor not an inch from Callie's nose. The dog never even woke up, but the edge of the metal picture frame hit with such force that it cracked a ceramic tile and left a hole in it, and shattered glass covered the dog's back and the floor. Another time a can of shaving cream fell off an open shelf in this same upstairs bathroom. It was sitting at the back of the shelf with other items in front of it and on either side. It fell with unbeliev-able force, shattering the plastic cap.

I spent a couple of years stripping wallpaper and painting. A number of times as I stood in the downstairs bathroom in front of the sink, when no one else was home, I felt a tap on my shoulder. I never thought much about it except that I remember thinking it was silly, perhaps a muscle twitch or spasm. I forgot all about it until my psychic guest's visit. As she was leaving, she told me that mine was the first haunted house she had visited. And then she said she wanted to know one thing: "Have you ever been home alone and felt like someone tapped you on the shoulder?" The hair stood up on the back of my neck.

One Saturday as I stood in front of the same bathroom sink, with the door at my back open and a clear view of the kitchen behind me through the mirror, I distinctly saw a man dressed in a light-colored shirt and blue pants stride across the room. I thought it was Mark returning from an errand, so I followed him into the dining room. No one was there. I searched the house but found no one; I tried to convince myself that it was just my imagination.

But oddities and coincidences continued, with marbles in particular. I know a number of Helenans who have unintentionally collected marbles, one at a time, over a period of years. The marbles suddenly appear in their homes for no apparent reason. Historic architect Herb Dawson, for example, lived in a house on Hillsdale in South-Central Helena that had a dark history. He admits that it was a scary place, but the most unsettling thing was that marbles kept showing up, especially on the front porch and around the living room radiator. A number of residents in Virginia City have had this experience, too.

We found a red cat's eye marble on the floor of the den in my house—just after I had thoroughly vacuumed the floor. Another time a very old marble appeared on the stairway—again, just after a thorough vacuuming, so perhaps I was knocking them loose from little-noticed nooks and crannies, but then we found an odd green cat's eye marble in the basement. A few others of different kinds and vintages have also appeared in the heating returns. I like to think that these marbles, like the tales collected here, are little leavings from another time, *spirit tailings*. ❋

Virginia City Tailings

George Lane's mummified foot and cane, post WWII. Montana Historical Society Photograph Archives, Helena.

Virginia Slade

TURBULENCE AND VIOLENCE CHARACTERIZED MONTANA's early gold camps. In particular the dark period of lawlessness between late 1863 and early 1864 fills a controversial chapter of the state's history. With the first gold strike at Grasshopper Creek in 1862, a diverse population began to flood into the area. This diversity grew as new strikes drew miners, merchants, and all manner of itinerants from faraway places to the remote fringe of the western frontier.

On the heels of the strikes at Grasshopper Creek where the town of Bannack sprang up, and at Alder Gulch where Virginia City was the main settlement, gold dust flowed freely in makeshift saloons and shops, and patrons had to keep a careful eye on dishonest shopkeepers. Dance hall proprietors swept the floors to collect the dust drunken miners spilled; enterprising merchants covered their rough log counters with strips of carpet, burning them when it was time to move on. They garnered substantial sums of gold dust that collected in the pile. Goods were expensive, entertainment surprisingly plentiful, travel was dangerous, and at least according to most contemporary accounts, the local population lived in terror of frequent robberies and murders along the primitive roads.

Before the creation of Montana Territory in late spring, 1864, there was little law enforcement. Attorney Wilbur F. Sanders and other members of the early community formed a vigilance committee after the makeshift trial, conviction, and hanging of George Ives at Nevada City in December of 1863. The actions taken to curb violence that followed the gold rush mentality are still a topic of earnest debate, but the fact remains that some two-dozen local executions at Bannack, Virginia City, Nevada City, and in other smaller communities were carried out within a matter of weeks. Some of the men convicted were certainly guilty, but others may have only been in the wrong place at the wrong time. One victim was a minor miscreant

The Slades' stone house along the toll road into Virginia City. Dabney Otis Collins, photographer (1951). Montana Historical Society Photograph Archives, Helena.

murdered by mob passions run amok.

The last hanging carried out by the Vigilantes in Virginia City was that of Captain Joseph A. "Jack" Slade, a character described by some as the consummate Dr. Jekyll and Mr. Hyde. Thomas Dimsdale, Vigilante sympathizer and chronicler, opens his account of Slade's hanging in *The Vigilantes of Montana* with this anonymous couplet:

> Some write him a hero, some a very knave;
> Curses and tears are mingled at his grave.

Slade's reputation followed him partly because the short, red-faced freighter made sure that tales of his exploits circulated among the saloons. How many notches he actually had on his gun is speculation, but Mark Twain, who met Slade before he came to Virginia City, wrote in *Roughing It* that the little bully claimed twenty-six killings. His most infamous deed was the killing of Jules Beni, who by all accounts was a very bad character, in retaliation for multiple bullets Beni put into Slade. After miraculously recovering from the grievous wounds Beni inflicted, Slade offered a $500 reward for the big French Canadian. A successful tracker brought him in and herded Beni into a corral where Slade reputedly emptied a revolver, rifle, and shotgun into his rival's non-vital parts, taking care not to finish him off. Before Beni's eyes glazed over for good, Slade sliced off both his victim's ears and held them out for the dying man to see. Slade kept the dried up, wrinkled ears in his pocket as souvenirs he later used as collateral for whiskey in Virginia City saloons.

Slade's other side was just as extreme. Reputedly, he once rescued a woman whose husband had been murdered, tracked down the two killers, and put an end to them both. Slade took the widow and her two children home to his house, sold their ranch, procured stage tickets home to Omaha for all three, and presented them with more than five hundred dollars he had taken from the pockets of the killers. But in 1861 Slade's exploits eventually got him fired from a well-paying job with Ben Holladay's Overland Stage Company and in 1863, Jack and his beautiful wife, Virginia, rode into the dusty streets of Virginia City on their high-strung thoroughbreds.

Virginia Slade was in some respects the antithesis of her husband; in other ways, she was his equal. Tall, full-figured and raven-haired, Virginia was a striking woman. She carried a revolver under her skirts, could shoot with the best marksmen and cuss like a miner. Although she may have been of questionable reputation before her marriage to Jack, the folks of Virginia City admired and respected Virginia in spite of what some of them thought of her husband. And Virginia was a model wife, loyal and devoted to her husband despite his behavior.

The Slades kept a ranch in the Meadow Valley seven miles north of town and collected tolls from travelers along the section of the Bozeman Road that wound down into Virginia City. Slade built a large stone house with a pole-and-sod roof near a sparkling spring that bubbled out of the mountainside. Virginia, an expert cook, served delectable meals on fine linen set with silver. Dressed in beautiful silk dresses that she made herself, Virginia Slade shone like a diamond among the simple, homespun settlers.

She was an avid horsewoman, too. The Slades loved to race their fast thoroughbreds down Virginia City's streets. On Sundays, Wallace and Jackson Streets were roped off for this purpose, and people came from miles around to pit their fastest horses against Slade's Old Copperbottom and Virginia's coal-black Billy Bay. Her Kentucky-bred stallion, once owned by American Fur Company trader Malcolm Clarke, was a wonder to behold. Billy Bay's raven-haired mistress sat tall in the saddle, riding astride like a man while her voluminous skirts billowed out behind her.

Slade, however, in time outlived his welcome in Virginia City. Sober he was tolerable, but drunk he was a menace, riding his horse through shop windows, shooting wildly in the streets, and scaring the town's residents. The property damage he caused was extensive. The end of the townsfolk's tolerance came in March 1864 when Jack and his cronies, after a night of wild, destructive carousing, upset the town's milk wagon, sending the precious supply down the hillside. The children of Virginia and Nevada Cities went thirsty that day thanks to Slade, who thought it all a great joke. The residents were not amused. The vigilance committee held a swift meeting and a brief trial. They took a course of action for which posterity has sometimes condemned them: Slade was sentenced to hang for little more than disturbing the peace. The executioners led Slade to the gate at the Elephant Corral on Cover Street behind present-day Rank's Drug Store. They then strung him up with Beni's ears still in his pocket.

A friend of the Slades had ridden out to Meadow Valley to warn Virginia, and the men at their grim task feared her powers of persuasion. They recognized the necessity of speed. As Slade blubbered his protests, the crate upon which he stood was kicked from beneath his feet and as he swung, someone shouted, "Mrs. Slade is coming!" The crowd was hushed. All heads turned towards the road up the hill. In the uncanny silence, pounding hoofbeats and a cloud of dust mixed with powdered snow announced the arrival of Virginia Slade, galloping frantically down the road on Billy Bay. She brandished her revolver as she rode hell-bent for the life of her husband. But she was too late.

Mrs. Peter Ronan, then a small child, never forgot the terrible moment. Nearly seventy years later when she was an old woman and herself a widow, Mary Ronan told her daughter, "My heart ached for Mrs. Slade. I slipped away from home, determined to tell her how sorry I was for her. I found her sobbing and moaning over a stark form shrouded in a blanket. I stood beside her for a moment, trembling and choking, then I slipped away unnoticed."

Harriet Sanders loaned Virginia a pair of black stockings—white being the fashion of the time—to wear for the funeral so that the widow could dress all in black. Mrs. Sanders later confessed that she attended the funeral more for curiosity than sorrow for the fate of Jack Slade. The Baptist minister was to preach a sermon, and the townspeople wondered what he would say about the deceased. The preacher began, "It has been my practice for the past thirty years when preaching funeral sermons to make little or no reference to the dead, and I will not digress from my usual habit." And he did not mention Slade throughout the entire service.

Virginia Slade's venomous rage for what the Vigilantes had done to her husband was frightful. She refused to have him buried where people had treated him thus. Legend says she had Jack sealed in a zinc-lined coffin filled with the whiskey that had been his undoing and when the snows melted, she took him to Salt Lake City for proper burial.

Helena businessman Charles W. Cannon years later told how Virginia took the mistaken notion that he had been a Vigilante and was in large part responsible for her husband's hanging. Cannon, at the time of Slade's execution, worked at a Virginia City mercantile. It was a long, narrow log building with tables down the center piled high with coats, pants and shirts. One day a man rushed into the store yelling, "Charlie, Mrs. Slade is coming!" Cannon dove under the last table at the back as Mrs. Slade came in the front brandishing a big powder and ball six-shooter, which she knew how to use. Up and down the aisles she went, swearing vengeance as Cannon narrowly escaped out the back door.

The next day Cannon had to make a trip to Salt Lake City for the firm. He got the last seat on the departing stage. As he settled in, he looked around and to his horror, Mrs. Slade was seated directly behind him wearing her six-shooter. It was an uncomfortable twenty-mile ride to the next stop, where Cannon paid a fellow passenger $20 to exchange seats.

Virginia Slade moved into town and opened a millinery shop. A year later, she married gentleman gambler Jim Kiskadden, a friend of her husband's, and moved to Salt Lake City. They soon divorced because, as Kiskadden discovered, only the devil himself could live with her.

The Slades' old stone tollhouse in the canyon along the little-used Bozeman Road stood vacant and fell into disrepair over the decades. Rattlesnakes slithered over the stones by day, bats circled at dusk, and creatures of the mountain skittered in and out the windows. The few travelers along the road did not tarry there, for tales of Slade's return, a raging, murderous apparition, fed their imaginations. Horse thieves fueled its haunted reputation. They murdered a miner there to further discourage visitors, making the meadow an even safer place for thieves to rendezvous. The haunted tollhouse was a clever ruse.

Old-timers may discount the ghost of Slade hovering near the ruined stone house, but anyone who has spent time in Virginia City knows about the fate of his beautiful wife. In earnest the locals will describe, as a chill creeps over the spine and gooseflesh prickles the skin, how sometimes the moon casts a silver light across the hillside northeast of town. On those rare occasions when the air is very still, the sound of hoofbeats in the distance pierces the quiet evening. Closer they come and then a cloud of dust appears high up along the road in the purple shadows. Out of the whirlwind, thundering down the hill, the ghostly form of Virginia Slade emerges from the shelter of the hillside into the moonlight. Her black skirts billow out behind her, her raven hair is loose, and the powerful black stallion gallops under her like a tempest, shaking his massive head in a spray of lather. A low moan gathers momentum and builds to a deafening scream. Her blood-curdling wails echo through the valley to the tops of the Tobacco Root Mountains. ✸

The Body in the Bathtub

It is an unassuming little place, a house that would go unnoticed unless there were some reason to seek it out. Tucked away on Cover Street, one of Virginia City's two unpaved residential lanes, it is just a short distance from Wallace Street where tourists amble along the board sidewalks. They stroll in the warm summer sun, peering through windows of imperfect, wavy glass at the collections of vintage artifacts. But visitors rarely venture to this neighborhood north of the main drag. Most are unaware of the high drama that once played out along the quiet street. At the Elephant Corral on the corner of Cover and Van Buren Streets, Captain Jack Slade breathed his last on a corral gate. That, however, is not the only scene that may make Cover Street an area especially charged with supernatural forces. There are other traumatic events that add to Cover Street's ghostly reputation. Among them are several emotionally charged episodes that affected the lives of three women who lived at different times in the small dwelling.

In more recent years, locals talked about the lady who lived in the house. From the 1940s through the 1980s, she made her home there on Cover Street. Most thought that this Virginia City matron, though respected and admired, had an over-active imagination because she rambled on about her bathroom. Her disconnected story had something to do with the bathtub, where a horrific, bloody apparition occasionally manifested itself. Lucille thereby earned herself a nickname, "Loose Wheel," and her hallucinations became well known to Virginia City's diehard residents.

Lucille sold the property, moved out, and its new owner, Tim Gordon, found tenants for the little house. If folks remembered the ramblings of "Loose Wheel," no one said any more about it. But recent research uncovered the troubled past of two of the home's former occupants, and proved that "Loose Wheel" was not crazy, only more sensitive than some. Her sensitivity must have created an uneasy existence for her in the little house.

Virginia City records show that the house first belonged to Martin Lyon, an early-day tailor who came to Virginia City with his family in 1864. Lyon and his wife, Anna, immigrated to Chicago—he was from England, and she from Ireland—and they later followed the gold rush west. Joining other settlers bound for the Montana gold fields, the Lyons came to Alder Gulch with their two sons, twenty-one-year-old Robert and twelve-year-old George, in a covered wagon. They reached Virginia City on July 24, 1864. Martin set up a successful tailor shop in Virginia City, where there was a demand for gentlemen's clothing and an abundance of gold dust.

One Saturday night in mid-January, 1865, as he made his way home from the shop, thieves struck Martin over the head and stole the week's profits that he carried in his pocket. Anna was in a frenzy, worried about his failure to come home that night, but a blinding three-day blizzard made searching impossible. When the snow finally ceased, searchers found Martin where his attackers had left him, his skull crushed and his pockets empty.

Martin's burial caused Anna further grief because, according to family legend, he was interred in the town's early cemetery ("Boot Hill"), where five men, hanged simultaneously on January 14 of the previous year, were also buried. Vigilantes had tried, convicted, and then hung them from the crossbeam of an unfinished shop. The building has been known ever since as the Hangman's Building. It still sits on Wallace Street with a diorama inside depicting this quintuple hanging.

There was disagreement among the locals and lawmen over the location of Martin Lyon's grave because of the heavy snowfall and because of the five other unmarked outlaws' graves atop the ridge. One of the five, Haze Lyons, may have contributed to the

Boot Hill in the early twentieth century. Montana Historical Society Photograph Archives, Helena.

confusion because of the similar last name. The stigma attached to Boot Hill soon prompted family members to move their deceased loved ones and re-inter them across the barren ridge top in Hillside Cemetery. The graves of the five outlaws buried on Boot Hill were undisturbed until 1907 when Mayor James Walker partially exhumed the body of Clubfoot George Lane, whose misshapen foot was readily identified. (The Walker family kept the foot as a souvenir and later donated the grisly object, with a piece of sock still attached, to Virginia City's Thompson-Hickman Museum. It can be viewed there today.) The five graves were then marked for the first time following eyewitness A. B. Davis' description of the order of their burials. No mention, however, is made of Martin Lyon's grave, and its location remains unknown.

Anna Lyon had come to the middle of nowhere on the western frontier with her husband and suddenly found herself alone. She had her sons, however, to console her for a while. They later married and moved on; both eventually left Montana, never

Frank and Amanda McKeen. Dick Pace, Golden Gulch: The Story of Montana's Fabulous Alder Gulch *(Virginia City, 1962).*

to return. Anna took in boarders and did domestic work to eke out a living, remaining in the house her husband had built until her death in 1896. Did the grief caused by the events in the winter of 1865 and the sadness of Anna's life linger on in the simple frame walls of the house?

Luther Buford bought the property after Anna's death and brought his bride, Nellie, to live there. Luther was a grocer in the Buford family's Virginia City store. The Bufords' occupancy in the little home was uneventful. In 1905 they sold the house to newlyweds Amanda and Frank McKeen. Frank was proprietor of the Anaconda Hotel and Saloon, today known as the Fairweather Inn. Frank was a colorful character, having sold whiskey over the bars of Virginia City's best saloons since the early days. He took over the Anaconda Saloon in the mid-1890s and expanded the original bar by adding hotel rooms, a restaurant, and a bowling alley in the basement. While his nice hotel was outfitted with the usual ladies' parlor, he maintained a back entrance to the bar for ladies of the "district." Frank's marriage to beautiful Amanda was a surprise to those who had long known the confirmed bachelor. Amanda and Frank had no children but seem to have done well until Prohibition. In 1918, the law ended Frank's bartending days, and he died the following year.

After Frank's death, Amanda stayed on in the house, despondent and depressed. But unlike Anna Lyon, Amanda could not survive alone. The following article, discovered in the *Madisonian*, March 30, 1923, perhaps explains Lucille's apparition:

MRS. MCKEEN SUICIDES

Neighbors were shocked Wednesday morning upon discovering that Mrs. Amanda McKeen had committed suicide by shooting. It was evident that she had been in unsound mental condition for some time. On Tuesday she went to Butte, supposedly for the sole purpose of purchasing a revolver. Returning Wednesday morning she went immediately to her home, entered the bathroom, placed the muzzle of the gun in her mouth and forced a shot upward in the brain. Undertaker Olson of Sheridan had charge of the funeral, which was conducted this afternoon, interment being in the Hillside Cemetery by the side of her late husband, Frank McKeen.

Records indicate that Amanda is buried at Hillside Cemetery next to her husband. The substantial granite marker noting the grave of Frank McKeen can be easily found along the road that runs through the neatly kept burial grounds. Although there is a place for her name next to his and a slight depression in the earth that would suggest a grave, Amanda's name was never added to the headstone. Her grave, like Martin Lyon's across the way at Boot Hill, is unmarked. ✸

Thus Would We Leave Her

A NEGLECTED REMINDER OF VIRGINIA CITY'S STORIED PAST sprawls across the unpaved corner of Idaho and Fairweather Streets. Built in 1876, this home's elegant gothic windows and solid stone walls, meant to withstand the test of time, are part of the legacy of wealthy pioneer merchant/banker Henry Elling. The once beautiful residence that now looms over its gentle hill-top adds an interesting dimension to Virginia City's charmingly archaic back streets. The Elling House is one of several gothic-style homes in the neighborhood, which reflect the trend to build homes in architectural styles—although out of fashion for the times—reminiscent of familiar places far away. Encircled by an ancient picket fence and stone wall barely visible for the tangled landscaping, its appearance fits the profile of the perfect haunted house. To gain perspective of this rambling mansion, the visi-tor can climb the road north of town to Virginia City's Hillside Cemetery where the Elling family monument is a prominent fea-ture. This quiet vantage point offers a spectacular bird's-eye view of the family home and the town itself.

German-born Henry Elling was a self-made man in the truest sense and enjoyed more than his share of good fortune. He came to the United States in the late 1850s to join a brother who had settled in Missouri. Tales of the western gold rushes made him restless, but being a cautious man, he took heed of the warnings made by the early emigrant guides and decided to take his chances mining the miners instead of a fickle gulch. The enterprising young Elling worked his way west, taking odd jobs and learning English. With the money he had carefully saved, Elling bought a load of goods and a team of oxen. He lumbered into Virginia City, Montana Territory, in October of 1864. Min-ers were glad to open their fat buckskin pokes of gold dust to buy supplies at just about any price Elling asked. His business thrived, and by the time his goods were sold, he had made nearly $10,000 in gold dust and nuggets.

Elling needed to invest in more goods and exchange his gold dust for currency, but being the prudent man he was, he worried about transporting so much wealth at a time when thieves regularly preyed on travelers along the roads heading out of this rich mining town. He had limited options. He could pay a private assayer a handsome sum to convert his gold; he could pay Wells Fargo an exorbitant ten percent of the total value to send it out of the territory; he could ship it via steamboat out of Fort Benton to the "States"; or he could take the gold himself. Although travel with such a cargo was a dangerous undertaking, Elling was reluctant to let it out of his sight and unwilling to pay shipping fees. So he devised a scheme. He divided his gold into two packages and stowed them in an old pair of boots, tying them together by their ears. He slung them over his shoulder and bought himself a new pair of boots to wear. On the stage to Omaha he complained loudly to anyone within earshot that his feet were very tender and unused to the new boots, and that he had to carry his old ones in case his new ones became unbearable. All along the way, Elling periodically changed his boots to give the impression that his poor aching feet were in need of their old familiar coverings. In this manner, Elling traveled with $10,000 unmolested.

In the next decade, as a merchant, Elling made a tidy sum. He also developed an uncanny knack for determining the weight of dust and nuggets. He could tell to the fraction of an ounce and to the penny, without using scales, exactly what a pile of dust was worth. Not only that, he could determine by its color from what part of the gulch the gold had come. Given these skills and his financial savvy, it was a natural step in Elling's career when he turned to banking in 1873. This proved profitable enough for

Elling to invest in other interests, and he became the wealthiest and most prominent citizen of Virginia City. He even served a stint as mayor. The safe in Elling's bank, still in the building today, always had a large store of the precious dust. Elling could pick and choose to whom he loaned his money since his bank was strictly a private enterprise.

Elling stuck to his little bank in Virginia City even though he eventually controlled seven Montana banking houses, including two he established in Helena and Bozeman. Before copper king William A. Clark rose to command his Butte empire, Henry Elling was financial overlord of Montana. He mined, farmed, raised livestock, and presided over state finances day after day in his tiny, remote Virginia City bank, sixty miles from the nearest railroad.

Henry Elling married schoolteacher Mary B. Cooley, daughter of a Madison County pioneer, in 1870. The couple had ten children, seven of whom reached adulthood. When Henry Elling died in 1900, his sons took over the banking business and Mrs. Elling stayed on in the house on Idaho Street. Mrs. Elling was a person of character and integrity, and according to locals she may have felt badly for some of her neighbors whose financial circumstances had been hurt by the actions of her banker husband. Not that Elling was a bad sort, but the nature of his banking interests sometimes forced him to put business ahead of sentiment. Even today folks remain ambivalent about this town father, but Mary Elling appears to have tried to mend some of the fences broken by her husband. After his death, she donated money to support the construction of the Episcopal Church, built in 1902. She also built an addition onto the back of her house to serve as a ballroom, and when she gave large parties, she opened it to the public as an offering of apology to those in the community affected by her husband's foreclosures.

Mary Elling died on Christmas Eve in 1924. Her obituary

in the *Madisonian*, January 2, 1925, had this to say following her funeral held in the lovely church she helped to build:

> The flowers were many and beautiful, but not more beautiful than the face that rested so peacefully among them. Beautiful in life, beautiful in death.... Thus would we leave her, and in memory keep her, as sweetly reposing among beautiful and fragrant flowers.

The house remained in the family until the 1940s. It served as a boarding house from the late 1940s until Charles Bovey acquired the property in 1953. The house was by then long vacant. Unoccupied and in disrepair, local children began to whisper about it. Did Mary Elling still walk the halls of her home? Certainly its rundown appearance fostered such stories. By the 1970s, the once-gracious home fit its role as the town's haunted house very well.

John Ellingsen, employed by Charlie and Sue Bovey to oversee their many Virginia City and Nevada City buildings, began to notice something odd about the house. It had its share of broken windows, but children throwing rocks or other missiles from the outside were not breaking them in the usual way. The windows were being broken *from the inside out*. Ellingsen periodically went to the house to repair damage, but confesses that he never felt comfortable there. He couldn't shake the feeling that someone was watching him, and he always finished his work as quickly as he could.

When local children broke into the house, it was Ellingsen's job to board up the ballroom door to prevent unwanted visitors. Ellingsen set out to secure the house. Taking some boards and his hammer and nails, he gathered his courage. Once inside, he reached the ballroom door at the far end of the house, took up a board and held it in place. As he drew back his hammer to pound the first nail, something grabbed his wrist and held it. He tried again, drawing back his hammer. And again something prevented his hammer from coming down on the nail. Try as he might, he could never get a good shot at the first nail. Ellingsen gathered up his tools and got out as fast as he could, and did not go back in the house again for many years. The message was quite clear that whoever or whatever grabbed his wrist did not want the door boarded up. Even though the house has been the subject of unwanted curiosity, Mary Elling seems reluctant to turn visitors away:

> Thus we would leave her, and *not only* in memory keep her, but in her home, in the house on the hill. ✹

Mother Irene
"Her children rose up and called her blessed."

Darkness settles over Virginia City. All the tourists have driven away or retired to the hospitality of their hotel rooms, residents have retreated to the comfort of their homes, and the curtain at the opera house has come down yet one more time. The wind carries an occasional sound from the tavern regulars at the Bale of Hale. But for that, the town is quiet, with night hovering like a lightweight summer blanket over the cabins and homes along Idaho Street. If anyone happens to be peering out a window at just the right moment, chances are that he might observe a black-robed figure gliding silently along the street. She (for all agree that it is a female spirit) moves with a purpose toward some destination: the nunnery (now the Bonanza House), the old hospital (now the Bonanza Inn), the Episcopal Church (the Catholic Church was long ago torn down). Residents and visitors alike say they have felt her eyes on them, watching through a window or sitting by the bedside; others claim to have seen her kneeling in a pew of the Episcopal Church. Some say the ghostly nun has visited them and healed their ailments.

Local tales of the shadowy visitor and reported sightings of her are sometimes tied to darker rumors of murder and violence. They say that a nun was murdered in Room #7 at the Bonanza Inn, and that she returns to relive the unholy act that took her life. Historical facts in no way corroborate this notion. The Bonanza Inn, however, does have a reputation as one of Virginia City's most haunted buildings. During its short tenure as a hospital in the 1870s, the *Montana Post* from time to time noted the deaths of patients there, and some patients from the mining camp certainly landed in the hospital due to violent encounters. In the 1940s, Charles Bovey began housing summer employees in the building. Now under state ownership, the facility houses staff, summer history camps, and occasional guests.

When Jill Verdon stayed in Room #7 one summer, two baffling incidents reinforced the Bonanza Inn's reputation as far as she was concerned. One day she left two bags of garbage by the door in her room to take out later. She locked her door and went to work. When she returned, the garbage sacks were on her bed. Later in the summer she noticed after getting into bed that three framed photographs she kept on the stand by her bedside had been turned upside down. Management insisted that no one had been in her room.

A state employee who stayed overnight in Room #7 in the late summer of 2000 recalled her own odd experience. She had just gotten out of the shower. Wrapped in a towel, she stepped out of the steamy bathroom into the bedroom. The smell of paint

Original Madison County Courthouse, now the Bonanza Inn (1989). Courtesy State Historic Preservation Office, Montana Historical Society, Helena.

and varnish permeated the room because the walls had just been painted and the wood floor refinished. As she took another step into the room, the paint smells suddenly disappeared completely. What remained instead was a very strong "nursing home" odor. There was no mistaking the smell. It took her back to her teen years as a candy striper in the geriatric ward of her hometown hospital. Another step forward took her into the odor of paint. She thought it very strange as she again stepped backwards into the unpleasant, familiar smell. As she stood there thinking about it, the smell of paint returned and the incident was over. She shuddered, thinking that over a century ago some unfortunate hospital inmate must have languished in this room, perhaps with consumption or some other terminal illness, until he finally expired.

Debra Munn has detailed other reported occurrences at the Bonanza Inn in *Big Sky Ghosts, Volume II*. These include newly-made beds torn apart, towels thrown on the floor, and other annoyances, but the most frightening experience happened to a crew member housed in Room #1 during the 1970s filming of the movie *The Missouri Breaks*. One night this young man stayed behind while other crew members went to Ennis for the evening. He had not been feeling well, and was resting when he heard a sharp knock at his door. "Who's there?" he called. No response. So he got up and opened the door. The long hallway was dark and empty. Then he heard the same ominous and insistent rapping at the window behind him. He shut his door, strode across the room, and pulled the curtains back. Nothing. As he peered out the window into the darkness, the sinister knocking began again at his door. He knew he had not imagined it because a little poodle, locked in the room across the hall while his mistress was out for the evening, was barking frantically. The young man found the experience so unnerving that he spent the night in his car and got a room elsewhere for the duration of the filming. After that, management supposedly locked Room #1 and left it unused long after this incident. Since the state assumed ownership of the Bonanza Inn, state employees and guests have occupied Room #1 without incident.

Spirits in the Bonanza Inn seem to extend their hauntings to the house behind it, the former nunnery now known as the Bonanza House. Debra Munn chronicles the reports of unearthly visitors, both male and female, inhabiting this house over the decades. In both these places and others along Idaho Street, for more than half a century the recurring thread in many accounts is the appearance of the black-robed sister. Several generations of people, unknown to each other, tell of the spectral "black robe" who keeps a bedside vigil. History suggests that there is a very good reason for the Idaho Street wanderings of the ghostly nun. She can be readily connected with a living counterpart who resided in Virginia City when it was teeming with rough characters and opportunists looking to make a fast fortune. Those who have seen her, or felt her presence, should consider themselves chosen, even blessed. For cloaked in the darkness, this transient phantom offers comfort and protection.

Among Virginia City's dynamic pioneer women were three Sisters of Charity who came to the mining camp in 1876 from their motherhouse in Leavenworth, Kansas, to open a hospital. They were Sister Louisa Carney, superior of the three; Sister Mary Leo Dempsey, a trained nurse; and eighteen-year-old Sister Irene McGrath, an unprofessed sister who had just completed a two-year novitiate and was to train under the older two.

This was not the first contingent of the black-robed sisters to come to Montana. Five sisters had come to Helena in 1869 where they founded St. John's Hospital, the first large medical facility in the Territory of Montana. They soon began a girls' academy, a boys' school, an orphanage, and a mental asylum, all in operation by the late 1870s. The primary mission of the Kansas order, founded in 1858, was to nurse the sick and teach children, but the sisters' activities extended to visiting and comforting the poor, the wayward, and the unfortunate. There were plenty of these in Alder Gulch.

The sisters came to Virginia City at the invitation of Father Francis J. Kelleher, to open a hospital for miners. They made the long journey from Leavenworth by train and stagecoach—nine days over roads axle-deep in mud—to what might have seemed to a young woman from Kansas the most remote corner of the world. The sisters arrived to find Virginia City a rough and rude place, stinging over the loss of the territorial capital to Helena the previous year. But Virginia City was still the county seat, and its brand new Madison County courthouse was a source of community pride. Construction of the new courthouse was fortuitous for the sisters, as they purchased the former courthouse—a primitive building with a tall false front—and converted it into several hospital wards.

St. Mary's Hospital opened in 1876. All Saints' Church, established by Father Kelleher, lay to one side on the corner of Jackson and Idaho, and to the other side a few doors down, the Bucket of Blood Saloon served a boisterous clientele. (Neither of these buildings stands today.) Living quarters for the sisters were behind the hospital in a new clapboard-covered house built for their use.

The three sisters tirelessly attended to the tasks at hand. Although more than a decade had passed since the rush to Alder Gulch, there were still plenty of miners with an assortment of ailments. Victims of tuberculosis, pneumonia, and mining accidents filled the wards while the deadly specters of cholera and typhoid, spread through primitive water sources, haunted the population. The black-robed sisters drew and hauled well water, gathered their own wood and kept a fire burning in the hospital yard. A huge kettle of water always boiled for the endless laundry. They hung clean bedding over the mountainside to dry, or freeze, at the weather's whim. The sisters cooked patients' meals and sterilized instruments on a small cookstove. To help cover expenses, patients paid $10 to $12 a week for the sisters' care.

Father Kelleher saw that pretty young Sister Irene, with her sweet smile, had a winning way with the patients and thought her charm might extend to youngsters. He requested Sister Louisa's permission to have the younger woman teach a catechism class to Virginia City's wild Catholic youngsters. Parents were delighted to have this positive influence over their children, who spent their free time hanging around saloons, running wild in the streets, and imitating the uncouth miners.

Sister Irene was sadly familiar with Virginia City's streets and alleys and troubled places because she was the one who most often escaped the hospital routine to visit those in need around the mining camp. While her superiors attended to hospital administration, Sister Irene freely moved about the camp, to and from the church, visiting the needy, and rounding up her pupils for catechism class. Despite warnings that the camp might not be a safe place for a young woman to walk about alone, Sister Irene never gave it much thought.

By the late 1870s, the placer diggings at Alder Gulch played out and many of the unsavory characters who once might have posed a threat to Sister Irene's solitary wanderings had left. By 1879, the hospital had few patients. Its doors closed and the sisters moved on. Virginia City was sad to see the gentle black robes go, but according to their rules, "the Sisters of Charity were never meant to be ornamental."

Sister Irene, especially beloved by the good citizens of Virginia City, went on to become superior of St. Joseph's

Hospital in Denver, where her strict medical and surgical practices helped create a code of ethics for medical personnel of all Catholic hospitals across the United States. Elected mother superior of the sisters' community in Leavenworth in 1904, Mother Irene served until 1908 but later returned to Montana, first as superior of St. Vincent's Hospital in Billings and then at St. James Hospital in Butte.

Many years later in Butte, Mother Irene had a patient who was a longtime resident of Virginia City. The patient recognized Mother Irene, and confided that she had helped organize a group of Virginia City women who vowed to never allow the young woman to walk the streets of the mining camp alone. Each time pretty Sister Irene had gone out, one of the volunteers had closely followed her. The seasoned mother superior was taken aback, and touched by this secret display of concern for her welfare.

Mother Irene ministered to the sick, caring for her patients with sympathy, respect, and good cheer for more than fifty years. When she passed away in 1944 at age eighty-seven, a Billings doctor said, "If Mother Irene and her smile aren't in Heaven when I get there, I'm not going in!" Courageous, charitable, gracious, and always hospitable, Mother Irene began her long service in Virginia City, and so she has a very special bond with its residents. Still following the rules of her order, she is not an ornamental spirit. She comes to pay her debt for that long-ago act of kindness and concern by taking care of those who need her. ✺

Lightning Splitter

LIGHTNING SPLITTER SITS AGAINST A BARE HILLSIDE on Virginia City's west end, facing Jackson Street. The house takes its name from the gable roof that makes it seem taller that it actually is. The roof is large for such a small house, and a doorway in the gable end opens onto nothing, its porch long since removed. For all its small size and rather plain appearance, Lightning Splitter has a disproportionately large number of stories connected to it. Most people who have called it home report strange occurrences of one kind or another, but the experiences of each individual resident seem to be uniquely personal.

One resident saw a ghostly form sitting in a chair, another awoke from a frightening dream to find angry red scratches all over his back, several men reported being chased by a doglike creature en route to the house, and lights have malfunctioned for no apparent reason. One occupant reported that her kitchen telephone would ring when the phone in another room did not; no one was ever on the line. These things and a general feeling of unease in the house, especially in the kitchen, upstairs, and on the stairway, are Lightning Splitter's legacy. Local tales that the house, built in the mid-1870s, was at one time a brothel are unfounded, and stories that a child died violently there are rumors at best.

One occupant lived in the Lightning Splitter during a summer in the late 1990s while she ran a restaurant leased from the State of Montana at nearby Nevada City. She had a number of weird experiences in the house. Three times she returned to an empty home to find the screen door locked *from the inside*. Her children refused to sleep upstairs because they would return home to find that their beds and furniture had been moved around. Once, when she had left doors unlocked and the keys in the house, the tenant returned home to find the doors locked.

Another time she distinctly heard a loud male voice call her by name and say, "What do you think you are doing, M——?" A longtime Virginia City resident told her that the spirits were playing pranks because they wanted her to know that they were there. They succeeded.

Just before this woman had come to Virginia City for the summer, her beloved family dog had died. He was a very big, friendly dog and had been a loyal protector. Family members were heartbroken when the dog choked to death on a bone. While they lived in Lightning Splitter, all present in the house heard what sounded like a big dog on the porch, gnawing a bone. They would go to the door, and the noise would stop. But as long as they lived in Lightning Splitter, they found some comfort in the fact that their dog was there to protect them from whatever unpleasant spirits lurked in the house.

Longtime Virginia City resident Jerry Fox also lived in

Lightning Splitter (1989). Courtesy State Historic Preservation Office, Montana Historical Society, Helena.

Lightning Splitter for a while. Jerry knew all the stories, but nothing strange happened to him while he lived in the house until he finished putting a coat of paint on the faded wallpaper in the upstairs bedroom. He went to lunch and returned to find, to his utter amazement, that the paint had completely disappeared. The wallpaper, previously stained and discolored, looked brand new. He wanted to turn around, take the stairs two at a time, and run away for good from Lightning Splitter's eerie vibes. Being a practical kind of guy, though, he forced himself to examine the circumstances carefully and found his "ghost" in the realities of refurbishing an old house. As he plucked up his courage and went to inspect the wall, his home-repair ghost revealed itself. A table had blocked his view of the entire wall. As he walked around it to the other side, he saw that the new paint had loosened the old wallpaper, and each strip lay neatly curled on the floor where it had fallen. Underneath the old wallpaper was another layer of the same pattern, but in much better shape than what Jerry had just painted. ✸

The Cook's Helper and the Winsome Maiden

NANCY ALLEN, NANCY'S NEPHEW GARRY MAIN, and Karla Boyd are the gracious proprietors of the Bennett House Country Inn in Virginia City. The three take good care of their guests, allowing them privacy and access to the parlor and dining room of the historic home of pioneer Judge A. J. Bennett. Some are convinced that the judge and his wife occasionally revisit their former home. Locals and guests gathered in the parlor or the dining room have been startled to hear the floor in the empty bedroom above creak with the footsteps of an unseen visitor. But this story is not about the Bennett House. This story is about the Gohn House down the street on the corner of Idaho and Jackson where Nancy makes her home.

The Gohn House is a charming Victorian-era residence built in the mid-1870s, surrounded by its original, distinctive hairpin iron fence. The house—kitty corner from the Bonanza Inn—later sheltered one of the town's most prominent couples, George and Mary Gohn. Both George and Mary were born in Virginia City. Mary's father, Robert Vickers, arrived by stage-coach in 1865. He was the first to bring the news of President Abraham Lincoln's assassination to the isolated frontier town. George, born that same year, was the son of one of the early merchants and was reputedly the first white male born in Virginia City. The marriage of Mary Vickers and George Gohn in 1896 united two of the oldest pioneer families in Alder Gulch.

Mary and George bought the house on the corner of Idaho and Jackson in 1897. The couple lived their entire lives in Virginia City, where George operated a meat market and then was elected to county office. He served as county clerk and recorder from 1918 until his retirement in 1932. George died in 1935 and Mary stayed on in the house for three more decades. She passed away in 1971, two months after celebrating her 100th birthday. Throughout her life Mrs. Gohn was an extremely fastidious housekeeper. She insisted, for example, that her household help extract lemon oil from *fresh* lemons to polish the furniture. She required that the inside of the stovepipe be cleaned weekly and her floors thoroughly mopped more frequently than even the most finicky housekeepers might demand.

Mrs. Gohn's desire for housekeeping perfection apparently lingers. She seems reluctant to turn her kitchen over to a new mistress, supervising her domestic domain with as much rigor in death as in life. She may even be a bit jealous of Nancy Allen's culinary expertise. Nancy loves to cook. Her father, Charles Whitcomb Sweitzer, was an old-world master baker and chef, and Nancy inherited his creative genius. She delights in making specialties for friends and guests. One morning, Nancy was trying out a new recipe for quiche. She had broken her leg, and was hobbling around on crutches. The first quiche was ready to go into the oven, and Nancy planned how she would maneuver the oven door with her crutches. She put them aside so that she could bend down to open the oven door. As she was precariously poised to slide in the pie plate filled to the brim with the runny, uncooked quiche, she saw something out of the corner of her eye.

In a far corner of the kitchen stood a tall, thin woman, dressed in clothing that appeared to be from the flapper era of the 1920s. As Nancy balanced herself in front of the oven, it occurred to her that she had seen this person before in the same corner, but it had not registered until just then. She began to slide the quiche onto the oven rack. It didn't seem to want to go in right, but Nancy had to get it in the oven before she could turn around and deal with what she saw in the corner. She again tried to slide the quiche onto the rack. But someone had put the rack in backwards and the quiche slid back, spilling all over the floor. When Nancy turned around, the apparition was gone.

Nancy was disturbed by this incident, because it was the second time she had seen this tall, thin woman in the same corner of her kitchen. A visit to the public library turned up a photograph of Mary Gohn late in life. The woman in the picture was older, but she was unmistakably the same woman Nancy had seen. Mrs. Gohn had been trying to warn her that the rack was in backwards. She didn't want that quiche to fall on her clean kitchen floor!

The Gohn family may provide the key to a longtime Virginia City mystery, and also explain something Nancy experienced a decade ago. Mary and George had four children—three boys, and a girl, Martha Mildred, born in 1904. The *Madisonian* called the little girl one of the "brightest and most winsome little maidens ever in the city." In 1911 when Martha Mildred was six, she became gravely ill with peritonitis. Her doctors decided to take her to Butte for surgery. She seemed better after the operation, but suddenly took a turn for the worse and died. Her grieving parents brought her back to Virginia City for burial. According to her obituary in the *Madisonian*, February 2, 1911, there was a "great weight of sorrow on everyone in the town . . . and all felt the loss of the little girl who . . . was known to everybody and beloved by all." Businesses closed and school was dismissed so all could attend her funeral. Six little playmates were the honorary pallbearers as the casket was borne from the house to St. Paul's Church for further services. There she "reposed in a bower of lace and flowers." Afterward, a large procession of mourners, that included most of the town, escorted the little girl's casket to Hillside Cemetery and laid her to rest.

From time to time, locals and seasonal employees have seen a winsome little six-year-old near a yellow rosebush next to the costume shop and at various places around town. Over the decades she has earned a reputation for playing tricks on the actors in Virginia City's summer theater. Although locals have long speculated that this elusive little girl was a victim of the deadly 1918 Spanish Flu epidemic that claimed several thousand Montanans, research suggests that the ghost is Martha Mildred, paying visits around her old neighborhood.

Nancy had an odd experience that supports this conclusion. Ten years ago, before she came to Montana, Nancy had an apartment in Portland, Oregon. During the time she lived there, she and at least three other acquaintances had several strange encounters in this apartment. All saw a little golden-haired girl come bounding through a field of yellow flowers, a small black dog at her side. The child and her little dog came running across the room and disappeared through the wall.

Nancy now wonders if this little girl was somehow trying to bring her to Virginia City. She has not seen her since moving to Montana, but the description of Martha Mildred fits the vision. In addition, Nancy has found something else that leads her to believe the little girl is still around. Marbles scattered in the garden, and a trail of them leading from the yard into the alley, suggest that little Martha Mildred scampers around the neighborhood and plays hide and seek in the yard. The marbles, symbolic of the innocent little girl so beloved by the town, are all pure white. ✹

Nevada City Ghosts

HIGH ATOP A RIDGE IN THE LITTLE CEMETERY west of Nevada City, Montana, pioneers long dead lie buried in the sandy soil beneath the scrubby sage and prickly pear. When all the noisy tourists have gone from Alder Gulch and the long winter begins to set in, tumbleweed catches on the rough edges of the broken headstones, piling up forlornly against them. Below the ridge in the little town of Nevada City, the wind whistles along the unpaved streets and through the chinks in the uninhabited log buildings. But Nevada City isn't always as deserted or peaceful as it seems.

Montana legislator and General Mills heir Charlie Bovey figures prominently in the more recent history of Nevada City, once a booming settlement in Alder Gulch. Bovey began buying dilapidated buildings in Virginia City in the 1940s. One day he saw a long-abandoned cabin on fire in the nearby ghost town of Nevada City. Upon investigation, he discovered that Lester Stiles had set an historic cabin on fire because it was endangering his horses. Lester and his wife, Mary, had acquired Nevada City in the 1930s and Lester used the property to pasture his livestock. But the crumbling buildings and hidden foundation walls posed a real danger to the horses. Destruction of the historic cabin struck Charlie at the very heart of his passion for abandoned buildings. He felt compelled to save them. So Charlie and Lester struck a mutually beneficial deal and Charlie got the deed to Nevada City's dozen derelict buildings.

Over the next three decades, Charlie's love of Montana's past led him to rescue many endangered buildings across Montana. He moved them into Nevada City, placing them along the deserted streets. He and his wife, Sue, filled their Nevada City buildings with a diverse array of "collections of collections." These artifacts are evident everywhere in the Bovey properties, now owned by the State of Montana.

Charlie Bovey had an uncanny knack for being in the right place at the right time. Once, for example, he was in New York City when a city ordinance had just passed outlawing street vendors with hurdy-gurdy organs. Charlie happened by a factory whose business, run by the Molinari family, depended upon repairing these particular types of organs. The new ordinance put the company out of business. Charlie bought all the music machines on the premises, including the tools and parts with which to repair them. Many of the fabulous music machines that came from the Molinari Organ Works of Brooklyn, New York, are now on display at the Nevada City Music Hall.

Charlie's lifelong good luck began in England when he was just a toddler. According to a family story, the Boveys were visiting there in 1912. When it was time to return to the States, they booked passage for the crossing, but Charlie came down with whooping cough. The family was quarantined, had to forfeit their reservations, and booked passage on a later ship, which turned out to be fortuitous. The tickets they had to cancel were for the first and only voyage of the *Titanic*.

Charlie Bovey loved Nevada City. He enjoyed strolling along the board sidewalk, taking in his collections and absorbing the history of his old buildings. Time after time, Charlie had happened upon a building—as he had with Lester Stiles—just as it was about to be demolished, and used his powers of persuasion to trade for or buy the ill-fated structure. He moved some eighty buildings to Nevada City, placing each one carefully along the streets. The town today is a ready-made movie set; its structures represent different time periods and places from across Montana.

Nevada City is not only a ghost town, but it is also a good place for ghost hunting. Emotions ran high with the gold rush, and right along Nevada City's main street, the miner's court convicted George Ives of murder and hanged him from the ridgepole of an unfinished cabin. The incident in December 1863 served as catalyst to the forming of the Vigilantes a few days later. Such strong emotions cannot help but leave vivid imprints on a place. The diverse pasts and origins of other Nevada City buildings raise myriad possibilities for spirit inhabitants.

Nevada City was Charlie Bovey's private retreat. He loved it especially because it was his own creation, manufactured of weathered boards and pieces and parts of things that he had taken apart, put back together, and arranged to his satisfaction. He was at home there and spent hours walking the streets. Although Charlie had a beautiful home in Virginia City, he often stayed in the cabins behind the Nevada City Hotel. On June 9, 1978, Charlie suffered a fatal heart attack in Cabin #5. His presence lingers everywhere in his buildings, and those who knew him believe that he still walks the streets of his beloved Nevada City. That, however, is another story.

Since the state acquired the Bovey properties in 1997, state employees watch over the buildings in Nevada City during the tourist season and when the town is closed for the winter. Sometimes they stay in Cabin #5 because it is furnished and equipped for overnight guests. In fact, longtime Bovey employee and state building curator John Ellingsen lived in Cabin #5 from 1972 until his own Nevada City cabin was finished in 1977.

One recent spring evening before the tourist season, Virginia City was hosting an Elderhostel. John and state employee Klaus Mackensen were conducting a "ghost walk" with some of the senior citizens. They came to Nevada City and as they approached Cabin #5, John told the group that he had lived there and had a good story to tell about something that happened to him during his stay. Klaus looked surprised and said that he, too, had a story about Cabin #5.

Klaus began by describing his residency in Cabin #5. It was early spring in 1999 and tourist season was weeks away. Nevada City was still closed tight and vacated for the winter. One night he was awakened by the sound of someone in heavy boots, unmistakably cowboy boots, walking along the board sidewalk that runs parallel to the highway. The heavy footsteps began at one end, and Klaus could hear them slowly moving towards the front of Cabin #6 near the center of town. Klaus quickly pulled on some clothes, and as he stepped out the door into the chilly air, he could hear the boots—clomp, clomp, clomp—slowly moving down the boardwalk. As he got to the visitor's gate, he could still hear the footsteps, but when he pushed through the stile and stepped onto the boards, there was only quiet.

John was visibly shaken. He admitted incredulously to the group that the exact same thing had happened to him. He had been sound asleep when his dog began to growl. John sat up with a start and heard the unmistakable clomp, clomp, clomp of heavy boots down at one end of the board sidewalk. The steps came closer and closer as he listened, and at last passed by. After his dog settled down and all was silent, he cautiously slipped outside. He crept to the gate, but no one was there. There is only one difference in the two stories. When John heard the heavy clomp, clomp, clomp, it was the dead of winter and a heavy snow was falling. When he got to the sidewalk, there were no sounds, and there were no footprints in the snow.

Perhaps Nevada City's most actively haunted structure is the two-story log building, today the state-operated Nevada City Hotel. In the 1860s one section of the building was a stage stop at Gaffney, a small settlement south of Twin Bridges, Montana. Its rough, primitive log walls, open porch across the front, and adjacent saloon recall a time long ago when a light in the window signaled a welcome respite for road-weary travelers. Bovey took the building apart, moved it to Nevada City, and rebuilt it on the site of the original 1860s Nevada City Hotel. At the back of the old stage stop, he attached a two-story dormitory from the Canyon Hotel at Yellowstone Park that once housed seasonal employees. The building dates to circa 1912. Today its rooms are the hotel's guest rooms, with accommodations for modern tourists.

The Boveys started and operated the modern hotel business at Nevada City, and visitors through the years have related plenty of odd incidents at the Nevada City Hotel. In the summer of 1999, the desk clerk told about one eerie episode that had occurred a few weeks previous. A gentleman had stayed the night in Room #11, and the next morning the desk clerk asked the guest if he had slept well. The guest informed the clerk that he hadn't.

"That woman in the room next door," he said, "cried all night long. I hope that she is okay. She was so upset. I didn't sleep at all, but I am more concerned about her. Do you know what was wrong?"

This was not the first time the desk clerk had heard such a complaint. He simply nodded and informed the man that there had been no guest that night in Room #12. The crying woman is an ongoing presence whose wailing has repeatedly annoyed guests. Nor is she the only unseen visitor.

Nevada City's uninhabited buildings and period authenticity make the setting ideal for film productions. *Little Big Man* with Dustin Hoffman is among the famous movies filmed there. In February 2001, a Global Stage production crew made two educational films at Nevada City: Edgar Allen Poe's *Ligeia* and Henry Ibsen's *Enemy of the People*. A scene of the latter was scheduled to be shot in the saloon at the Nevada City Hotel. Preparations began well in advance of the crew's arrival. In January a few weeks before the filming, state employee Marge

Nevada City Hotel. Tom Ferris, photographer (Sept. 29, 1998). Montana Historical Society Photograph Archives, Helena.

Antolik was working in the saloon when she had what she described as a "playful reminder" that she was not alone in the old hotel. Her experience served as a preface to the welcome that was to come.

It was Marge's job to take a preliminary inventory of the saloon. It was very cold and dark in the deserted hotel in the dead of winter. She set her flashlight, tape measure, and other items on the bar. As she went about her work, she used the flashlight several times, always replacing it on the bar. She then turned away to inventory artwork hanging on the wall. When she again needed more light, she reached for the flashlight, but it was not there. She searched for quite a while, finally gave up, and turned to go back to work. She glanced back at the bar and there was the flashlight, precisely where she had left it. She stayed to finish the inventory but with the conviction that she was not alone.

The Global Stage crew came in a few days later to film the saloon scene on one of the coldest nights of the year. The temperature dipped below zero, and the old log building offered meager comfort at best. The guest rooms and corridors upstairs and down were all locked. Perhaps fifty people crowded into the bar, including some seventeen cast and crew members and a number of local "extras." According to John Ellingsen, "The director called 'quiet on the set' and the camera began to roll. Everyone was holding their breath, afraid to make a sound, when suddenly there were footsteps in the room above. 'Cut! Who's up there?' yelled the director. I, along with several other crew members, rushed upstairs. The hall was dark, and when I unlocked Room 7, the room over the bar, it, too, was dark, cold, and no one was inside!"

The floor kept creaking, slowly and deliberately, during the entire time the crew and actors were in the hotel. It was even captured on tape. Finally the production crew finished. As everyone filed out, one young lady felt a distinct tap on her shoulder as she walked along the board sidewalk in the dark. She brushed at her shoulder and turned around, but no one was there.

Marge was there during the filming to supervise the film crew. "I could hear the pacing back and forth upstairs," she said. "It was unmistakable that the spirit was an unhappy one, not pleased with the intrusion of so many in what is usually the undisturbed time of year."

Collections curator Pat Roath was at the door of the hotel at 7 AM the next morning to clean up after the film crew had finished. As she stood there about to unlock the door, she heard the footsteps coming from inside the locked building. She wondered who was in there. Once inside, the footsteps continued. They seemed to be coming from the main floor hallway, but when she looked down the hall, no one was there. It was definitely the sound of boots, cowboy boots, on a wooden floor. The weirdest thing was that the hallway was carpeted!

She said to herself, "Okay, I have to do this. I'll just get it done." Her instincts told her to get out—whoever or whatever it was didn't want her there. She hurried to finish her work. It took about an hour and all the while the insistent footsteps, boots on the wooden floor, paced up and down the carpeted hallway. Later in the morning, Pat returned to get some chairs. She was in the hotel lobby and, again, she heard the unmistakable sound of boots on a wooden floor in the carpeted main hallway. Pat says that ghosts do not usually bother her, but this was "very creepy."

Marge also heard the footsteps again when she came in later to clean and do a final inventory in the saloon. She heard the impatient resident in the back hallway: CLOMP! CLOMP! CLOMP! She also got the message: GET OUT! GET OUT! GET OUT! She wasted no time in doing her work, then locked the door and let the angry occupant have his peace and quiet. Although the identity of this spirit cowboy is a mystery, it is likely the same booted phantom that disturbed John and Klaus. It is not Charlie Bovey; he would never be so inhospitable. Besides, Charlie never wore cowboy boots.

Even in the summertime, when hotel guests sit out on the board sidewalk visiting, dusk washes over the streets and a chill sets in. Darkness creeps into the nooks and crannies of the old log walls. The buildings with their collective histories have stories to tell, and at least one resident who doesn't like to share the solitude. ✸

Butte Tailings

Steel headframe and hoist, Original Mine in Butte. Norman A. Forsyth, photographer (circa 1910). Montana Historical Society Photograph Archives, Helena.

Butte Mine Spooks

Butte was a lively gold camp during the 1860s, with dozens of miners' shacks strewn across the hills and gulches and a population typical of a hundred other fly-by-night boomtowns. Its gold proved difficult to extract, and water, required for placer mining, was scarce. Butte, though, would soon enough yield its destiny. In the mid-1870s experienced miners realized that Butte's potential lay in silver and copper, not gold. A well-respected upstart miner by the name of Marcus Daly helped develop Butte's immense potential for copper. New technologies, including telephones and electric lighting, created demands for this metal, and wealthy investors gambled wildly to finance mining operations. Butte rose quickly to prominence, taking a unique place in Montana as a huge urban industrial center essentially in the middle of nowhere. It became one of the toughest towns in America, the national birthplace of unionism, and a melting pot of every conceivable language and culture.

So famous were the mines of Butte, in fact, that New York officials loaded non-English-speaking immigrants with no declared destination onto trains bound for Butte as a matter of course. There was always work in the mines at Butte. Underground, the miners worked their shifts; above ground, soot blocked the sunshine, sulphur choked the air, and cyanide let nothing grow, even in the yard of copper king William A. Clark. And fear was part of life in Butte.

Every miner's family lived with the dark, nagging fears of occupational hazards: falling rocks, fire, electrocution, explosions, cave-ins, and the "miner's con"—tuberculosis or silicosis. Everyone feared the electric drills that constantly chewed into the rock and spit out the consumptive dust, dust that eventually corrupted a miner's lungs. The drills earned their sobriquet, "widow makers." The steel headframes that loom even today against the horizon like hulking skeletons earned their own grim nickname: gallows frames. They supported the hoists above the mineshafts where waiting cages carried the men deep into the bowels of the hill. Clanging and shuddering all the way down to the bottom of the hole, the men uneasily entrusted their safety to the heavy cables, levers, and cages. Miners tired to the bone fought that metallic grinding as it echoed in their dreams. Heavy machinery is the heart of successful mining, but its legacy is fear and death.

Butte lured her men like a siren with promises of the American Dream, then crushed them in her metal, suffocated them in her tunnels, killed them with her dust. Most old timers who have spent any time underground will tell you that there are spirits in the tunnels that appear in the form of shiny eyes gleaming in the pitch dark. They float through the tunnels, checking on the places where they used to work, watching the progress of the new miners who replaced them.

Waino Nyland came with his parents to Butte from Finland just after the turn of the twentieth century. Nyland wrote an account of his Butte childhood that appeared in *Scribner's Magazine* in May 1934. He remembered that the first disaster his family experienced after arriving occurred when a lever broke on a hoisting engine as a cage was taking four men down into the mines. The cage fell, plummeting twenty-two hundred feet, ripping out the shoring timbers all the way down and butchering the unfortunate riders. The accident destroyed a whole mine, rendering it useless, never to be used again. The bodies of the four men, one of them Nyland's next-door neighbor, came out of the wreckage in pieces and were sorted out as well as conditions allowed. The men's spirits, according to Nyland, still haunt the mine. If you look down the shaft when the time is right on certain days, four pairs of lonely eyes stare back at you, looking up from the bottom of their deep, dark grave.

Unlike Nyland, most miners do not like to talk about ghosts, but all Butte miners have heard unexplained noises deep in the mines, had shovels or buckets disappear, and they all know to watch out for the white goat that is said to roam Anaconda Hill. He can turn up anywhere because all Butte mines are connected, and sneak up from behind. If you are too close to the edge of a shaft, he'll butt you right in. Then there is the phantom ring. Every hoisting engineer has answered a ring for a hoist up where no one is working. If he sends a cage down in answer to the ring, it invariably comes back empty.

A miner named Jerry, his partner, and the "shifter"(who provided transition from one shift to the next) went down fourteen hundred feet to check out a small cave-in that had occurred on the previous shift. They reached the site and discovered not only that the clean-up had yet to be completed, but also that the electric lights were out. The last shift's men must have been drunk, they thought, not to have done their work. The shifter informed them that there had been a ring at twelve hundred feet during that last shift, but no one had been there when the cage came down. Jerry's partner and the shifter went back up to find an electrician to fix the lights, leaving Jerry to shovel rock.

No sooner had the men disappeared than Jerry heard a timber pop like it was going to break, a disconcerting but not uncommon sound. Then he heard water splashing. "What the hell?" thought Jerry, knowing there was no water down there. A rock then plummeted from the lagging above. Did someone drop it, or did it fall on its own? Then he heard the splashing again, and a "squish squish" like someone walking in water in gum boots. His lantern sputtered and Jerry thought to himself, "Where the hell are they with that electrician? They've been gone long enough."

Jerry returned to shoveling. His lantern sputtered again and dimmed, almost like someone was trying to extinguish it, then it brightened and evened out. Jerry began to think about how the engineer got that ring for the cage at twelve hundred feet and no one came up. Jerry kept shoveling and tried not to think about being alone. His lantern sputtered again. He kept shoveling. Then Jerry felt a tap on his shoulder. His heart beat faster and he shoveled harder, not wanting to turn around. He felt another tap, more like a poke. Jerry swung around, and facing him there in the tunnel was a man with no arms or legs. His face was so smudged and caked with dirt, only his eyes shone in the lantern light. He looked like he had been caught under a rock in a cave-in.

Jerry turned around and fled toward the lights of the station. "But," he worried, "no one will be there, and what will I do?" The thing was right behind him, effortlessly keeping up with Jerry's labored running. *Right behind him!* As Jerry approached the station, he realized that the cage was there, as if waiting for him. Jerry rang for the hoist and the thing got on the cage with him. He pushed it off as the cage began its ascent, but the thing stayed right underneath, following the cage up. By the time the cage reached the top, Jerry lay on the floor in a heap, his blood thinned to ice water. According to Nyland, Jerry spent some time in the hospital and later took a job as a watchman. When people questioned him about his ordeal, Jerry went blank and told them to get the hell out of his way.

Mangled corpses and butchered pursuers are bad enough, but nothing compares to America's worst hardrock mining disaster. On June 8, 1917, a carbide lamp at the North Butte Mining Company's Speculator Mine ignited frayed electrical insulation in the Granite Mountain shaft. Fire spread, and carbon monoxide and other deadly gases swept through the tunnels, killing more than 160 men. Some died instantly, but others had time to scrawl poignant goodbye letters to their families in the darkness as the oxygen ran out.

A stunning monument on the hill overlooking the site of the disaster is fringed in facsimiles of their written words. The mine reopened in 1940, and for three miners who worked a first shift, it was a chilling experience. Once underground, the men heard the sounds of heavy breathing. And why wouldn't they? A tragedy like that in the Granite Mountain shaft—sealed for more than twenty years—left an indelible imprint of young men in their final hours, deep in the earth, gasping for air as the oxygen ran out. ❀

The Haunting of the Quartz Street Fire Station

THE MINING CITY OF BUTTE, MONTANA, has experienced some of the nation's worst disasters and mourned more than its share of fallen heroes. The Quartz Street Fire Station, today home to the Butte–Silver Bow Public Archives, is a significant landmark that rose in the aftermath of one of Montana's most tragic and devastating events. The station's first resident chief battled fires, city hall, and personal tragedies as he helped modernize the Butte Fire Department. Today, the building is an important legacy with a story worth remembering. And some say it is a story that the building and its past occupants will not let them forget.

The disaster that served as catalyst to the construction of Butte's Quartz Street Fire Station, and other fire protection improvements, came with no warning on January 15, 1895. Firemen answered a call to put out a fire in the South Butte warehouse of the Royal Milling Company. The firemen did not know that tons of blasting powder had been illegally stored in the nearby Kenyon-Connell Commercial Company and Butte Hardware Company warehouses. Flames reached the powder and the first terrific explosion blew the metal roof of the Kenyon-Connell building one hundred feet in the air, hurling some thirty-five people to their deaths. As passersby rushed to aid victims, two more blasts turned iron bars and metal pipes stored in the warehouse into deadly missiles that found targets as distant as a mile from the explosions. Searing oil rained down on the crowd. Sidewalks throughout Butte all the way to Walkerville glistened with broken glass from shattered windows. Body parts and flesh were flung in a wide radius from the explosions, and the site itself was a ghastly pile of twisted metal and dead horses.

Authorities counted at least fifty-seven deaths and more

Miners prepare to blast. Norman A. Forsyth, photographer (circa 1910). Montana Historical Society Photograph Archives, Helena.

than one hundred injured, but Butte's transient population and the complete annihilation of some bodies suggest the toll was much higher. Fatalities included eight children, a police officer, and thirteen of the city's paid and volunteer firefighters, as well as three of the department's best horses. Among the mangled victims were Fire Chief Angus Cameron (identified only by the belt that he wore) and Assistant Chief John Sloan. Sloan's younger brother Ed, also a fireman, was killed in the blast, and their father, John Sloan, Sr., who knew about the stored powder, was mortally injured rushing to the scene to warn his sons. Flying debris killed Joseph Leveque as he drew water from the well in his back yard; other debris paralyzed his young son. As Leveque's funeral was being held a few days later, Mrs. Leveque gave birth to a child, adding another member to her already destitute family. Hardly a person in Butte was untouched by the devastation, and for decades thereafter, citizens reckoned their residency in terms of years before or after the "Big Explosion." Only the Speculator Mine fire in 1917 eclipsed this horrendous calamity.

The three firemen who escaped the cataclysmic event had been detained en route to the alarm. One was Peter Sanger, an Ohio native of German extraction and an experienced fireman. Although trained as a barber, Sanger was a veteran of Leadville, Aspen, and Denver, Colorado fire departments. He and his wife, Margaret, came to Butte in 1888, where he had worked as a miner, barber, and volunteer fireman before joining the paid force in 1895.

Sanger's contributions to the safety of Butte were significant. When he began his tenure as chief in 1899, Butte's force consisted of fourteen paid firemen. Sanger immediately hired more firemen, organizing the Quartz Street Station as the main station and adding the Caledonia Street and Arizona Street Stations. The station on Quartz Street, built in 1900, housed twenty-two men, the chief, and the chief's family. Chief Sanger built a tower near the Quartz Street Station and required his men to perform needed drills; he provided them with a gymnasium; he secured better living quarters for the men; he advocated the firemen's pension bill; and throughout his career he was active in state and national firemen's associations. Finally, Chief Sanger demanded that the city institute a more thorough system of electrical alarm boxes, urging one be installed on nearly every street corner. By 1905, the Butte Fire Department had forty-one members and each station was equipped with its own horse-drawn apparatus. Then in 1912 a series of five very serious fires in the business district gave Sanger opportunity to press for more modern, motorized equipment, and the city council authorized him to purchase Butte's first three motorized fire vehicles at a cost of $11,000.

Despite a charmed career as fire chief, several crises marred Sanger's personal life. Margaret suffered with cancer for several years and died at the family apartments in the Quartz Street Station in 1904. His wife's death was a blow not only to Sanger and his two children, Hazel and Leslie, but also to the department. Margaret had endeared herself to her husband's men for her acts of kindness and consideration. A long procession of firemen and admirers bore her remains from the station to St. Patrick's Catholic Church. Two carriages were filled with floral offerings, and flowers from friends completely covered her grave.

Two years later Chief Sanger and his son, Leslie, rushed to the bedside of eighteen-year-old Hazel. They had been summoned to the normal school at Dillon where Hazel, a student there, had fallen gravely ill. The young woman, in delicate health since the death of her mother and tended by a private nurse, did not seem especially ill, but she died of peritonitis forty minutes before her father and brother arrived by train at the Dillon depot.

Peter Sanger grieved, then remarried in 1908, and he and his second wife, Louisa, made their home in the roomy apartments upstairs at the Quartz Street Fire Station. Louisa must have keenly felt the family's past tragedies there in the Quartz Street rooms, and kept a vigilant eye on her husband from an upstairs window. Like Margaret before her and wives of other chiefs after her, she took up a post by the window time and time again to observe activities below and to wait for her husband's return. As one might expect of a fireman, the chief did not always return safely. He sustained several serious injuries between 1912 and 1915, and suffered from respiratory problems due to smoke and gas inhalation.

Louisa Sanger watches from the window at the Quartz Street Fire Station as the firemen test their net. Butte-Silver Bow County Public Archives, Butte.

In 1915 city administrators closed the Caledonia Street Station over Chief Sanger's strident protests. The Quartz Street Station was thus answering the other station's calls when he and three others sped to an alarm on January 11, 1915, in the new "Flying Squadron" fire wagon, Chemical Auto No. 5. The truck was going about forty miles an hour when it collided with a

Walkerville streetcar. All four occupants were thrown at least thirty feet. Sanger, not in the best of health due to his recent injuries, was the only person seriously hurt. Friends carried him in a semiconscious state to the Quartz Street Station, where the doctor diagnosed a brain concussion and hemorrhage. Although conscious, Sanger did not improve, and some weeks later he and Louisa took a train to San Jose, California, for surgical trepanning. He retained his faculties throughout the journey but did not believe he would survive the procedure. Just before the surgery, he told his good friend Chief Edward Haley of the San Jose Fire Department, "Do what you can for my wife. . . . I am in bad shape . . . and I feel that I will have to go over the hurdles." Haley promised and the two parted with a handclasp. Sanger did not survive the procedure.

Louisa Sanger brought her husband home to the Quartz Street Station where his body lay in state. Butte's firehouses were draped in mourning and flags across the city flew at half-mast. Hundreds came to the station to pay their last respects. The cortege made its way to the funeral service at St. Patrick's. The casket was borne on one of the old fire wagons drawn by semi-retired equine veterans, Tom and Jerry. A fireman led a third horse drawing the chief's empty buggy. All city officials who could be spared from duty attended the funeral "...as a mark of respect to the man who served the city so faithfully and well. . . ." Chief Sanger was a hero's hero who always said he would never send his men anywhere he would not go himself, and he never did.

Louisa was a loyal wife who stayed close to her husband throughout his ordeal, so it must have been difficult to lay him to rest next to the graves of his first wife and his daughter. Soon after, Louisa moved to Los Angeles, but the Sanger family tragedies claimed a last victim. Leslie Sanger died on October 3, 1918, a field artillery sergeant in service to his country during World War I; he was also buried in the family plot in St. Patrick's Cemetery. He left a wife, Nora, and two small daughters, Dorothy and Hazel, who last appeared in Butte in 1923.

Life went on at the Quartz Street Station for decades following the Sangers, housing several more generations of firefighters and chiefs. In 1981 the station became the new home of the Butte–Silver Bow Public Archives. Today, traces of its past remain, illustrating well the evolution of Butte's fire department. The stable where Tom, Jerry, and the other valuable fire horses received the men's care and affection remains intact in a dark corner of the semi-basement. The bays that first housed the horse-drawn equipment and later the shiny new engines are also unchanged. On this same ground floor, the kitchen where the firemen took their meals, the chief's office, and the numerous alarm boxes installed by Chief Sanger are all still in place. The alarms, however, have long been disconnected.

The building has a presence and dignity that fits its use now as the repository of Butte's memories. The decision to leave the building unchanged blends beautifully with its current adaptation. Some sense that the walls, having absorbed eighty years of adrenalin, as well as the amicable banter of the men who lived and worked within the shelter of the station, have their own memories. Those who work in the archives sometimes feel that the firemen never left, that they watch over their old familiar haunts downstairs. Some even say they *murmur* down there in the darkness.

Upstairs, the spacious, sunlit reading room with its sweeping tripartite window and vintage wooden floor was once the men's sleeping quarters, their empty lockers line one end of the room. The fire chief's apartment rooms harbor a welcome that is difficult to define. The director of the Butte–Silver Bow Public

Archives, pleased with this fitting use of the old building, is in tune with its quirks. She, Suzan Maloney, and Judy Strand all work upstairs and they can vouch for at least one of the station's idiosyncrasies. All three have heard, at different times, the disconnected alarm bells clang.

One day, while out in the parking lot, the director happened to glance up at the east window. She saw an older woman, drying her hands on a dishtowel, looking out over the parking lot to the street beyond. She thought that maybe she had imagined it until some time later she stumbled upon a picture of the very woman in the window. Peter Sanger was unknown to her, and so was Louisa. But the woman in the window was there nonetheless, dishtowel in hand, waiting for the men to return. ✸

Of Copper Kings and Other Things

THE METALS BANK BUILDING ON THE CORNER of Park and Main Streets in Butte is one of Montana's most impressive commercial structures. Designed by famous architect Cass Gilbert of New York and built in 1906, it shares some architectural features with the famed Montana Club in Helena (see "Montana Club's Urban Legend"), also designed by Gilbert at the same time. The two landmarks were pivotal buildings in Montana, constructed with new techniques that allowed multiple stories. Gilbert went on to design the famed sixty-story Woolworth Building in 1913, one of America's first true skyscrapers. Owners Robbie and Boyd Taylor have beautifully restored the Metals Bank Building to its original appearance. Imported and domestic marble and hardwoods recall the time when Butte was an industrial giant and copper reigned. The building's history and the site, however, are intertwined with some of Butte's darkest hours.

The ground floor of the seven-story Metals Bank originally housed the State Savings Bank. A previous building on this corner was the first site of the State Savings Bank where a tragedy occurred in January 1898. Bank president Patrick Largey, sometimes known as Butte's fourth copper king (after Marcus Daly, William A. Clark, and F. Augustus Heinze), took a bullet just above the heart and a second one in the forehead. He died soon after the shooting. Doctors reported that either wound would have been fatal.

The shooting took place nearly three years to the day after the great powder explosion, January 15, 1895, recounted in the previous chapter. The perpetrator of the crime that left Largey dead was one Thomas Riley, who held Largey responsible for a crippling injury. The explosion blew off Riley's left leg. Although some victims and their families had won court judgments against the companies, they were unable to collect. Riley, though, did not sue, and the Kenyon-Connell and Butte Hardware companies gave him $1500, which he promptly spent; he then demanded more. Though Patrick Largey owned stock in the hardware business, he had no personal responsibility for the disaster. Riley felt otherwise and badgered Largey for additional money and financial assistance. Largey helped Riley secure employment several times during the three years after the accident, but Riley proved an unreliable employee.

The *Butte Miner* of January 18, 1898, described Largey's funeral in minute detail. Mourners decorated St. Patrick's in black crepe and streamers, and Bishop John Brondel came from Helena to attend. Largey's wife and teenage daughter, grief stricken, "…gazed on the dead as though hoping to bring him back to life, by the intensity of their sorrows." A huge profusion of flowers was loaded onto a specially built platform and transported to the cemetery. Black horses draped in black netting drew the carriage bearing Largey's remains in the finest casket available—a model called the "grand chancellor" trimmed in silver and gold. The funeral cortege was a mile long. Thus came the end of the fourth copper king, a respected man, cut down in the prime of his life. Surely the hatred and violence that robbed him of a ripe old age would leave some kind of impression on the place where it happened, wouldn't it?

The fortunes, and misfortunes, of the third copper king, F. Augustus Heinze, are also a part of the history of the Metals Bank Building. Heinze was a dashing figure, brilliant, aggressive, and unscrupulous. Women adored him, and he lived a fast, colorful life. Heinze was a graduate engineer of German extraction who arrived in Butte at the age of twenty in 1889. He went to work for the Boston and Montana Company and quickly achieved great success, both professional and financial. He organized the Montana Ore Purchasing Company in 1893 and allied with William A. Clark. Heinze and Clark rose to challenge the political and economic power of the Amalgamated Copper Company, Marcus Daly's former operation, newly controlled by Standard Oil. The picture looked bright for Heinze at the turn of the century, but mining fortunes made quickly could be lost just as fast. Heinze's United Copper Company stock was mysteriously bought and sold, likely a calculated move by Standard Oil. This activity, as well as runs on Heinze's bank and his own mistakes, brought financial ruin from which he never recovered. Briefly married in 1910, Heinze died in New York City in 1914 of cirrhosis of the liver and massive hemorrhaging. He was only forty-five.

At the height of Heinze's legal and financial troubles, his mining fortunes financed Butte's $325,000 "skyscraper," the handsome Metals Bank Building built on the site of Largey's old State Savings Bank. Its seven floors today house a number of businesses, and the building's elevator, one of those marvelous relics from another time, still takes passengers up and down. While the elevator is perfectly safe, those who avoid close quarters find that the small, cramped carriage brings on claustrophobia. Decades of humanity, too, have left their traces in the form of a peculiar permeating odor that sometimes wafts over the passengers. A few report that the elevator refused to let them out on the desired floor, stopping instead between floors and getting stuck. Old elevators, though, sometimes behave that way, and those who prefer can opt for the stairs.

At night, when the old building rests from the bustle of the average workday, some say the elevator toils on. Up and down it travels, delivering unseen passengers to empty halls and locked offices. Perhaps Patrick Largey walks the lofty halls, riding up and down, or perhaps Heinze returns to the building, the only legacy he left in Butte, in search of an answer to weighty legal and financial problems. Or, perhaps the elevator responds to an even darker legacy.

From the 1920s through the 1930s, one of the most despised characters in the history of Montana had her offices on the fifth floor of the Metals Bank Building. Dr. Gertrude Pitkanen's back-alley abortions and illegal adoptions have made her infamous across the state. "Gertie" was a chiropractor whose first husband, physician and surgeon Dr. Gust Pitkanen, also had an office in the Metals Bank Building on the second floor. Gust, like his wife, was a well-known abortionist. Gertie operated her "maternity home" from the Metals' fifth floor until about 1940 when she moved to 115 Hamilton Street.

During Gertie's long career, she was arrested at least three times and charged with manslaughter for botched abortions. According to an article about "Gertie's Babies" in the Helena *Independent Record,* August 8, 1994, "she carried a little black book and all she had to do was open it and the judge would dismiss her case." Her second husband was a Butte detective. One of Gertie's several adopted children called her a mean and horribly abusive mother who even tried to force her adopted brother to sell his firstborn child. Gertie's secrets went with her to the grave in 1960; the full extent of her black market adoptions and their implications will probably never be known. Her longtime occupancy in the Metals Bank Building makes one wonder how many of Gertie's patients might have clandestinely ridden the elevator to the fifth floor under cover of night.

The Metals Bank Building remains a fabulous testament to Butte's multi-faceted past and a significant landmark. Its unsettling history contributes to the unique sense of place that visitors notice about it. Patrick Largey's violent end, the troubles of Augustus Heinze, and the dark deeds of Gertrude and Gust Pitkanen are ample reasons for spirits to roam its halls and for the empty elevator to travel up and down after hours. ✸

A Spook to Believe In

THE METALS BANK BUILDING ISN'T THE ONLY place in downtown Butte where the elevator goes up and down on its own. Doors that open and close, footsteps shuffling down the halls, books falling off shelves, a tall figure who roams the building, and an elevator with a mind of its own all figure in the tales and legends of the Butte–Silver Bow County Courthouse.

Most Montana towns have had their hangings, and Butte is no exception. Between 1889 and 1926, ten men faced the gallows in the jail yard next to the county courthouse. The execution of Anthony Vettere, hanged October 1, 1926, was the last and the most spectacular. Vettere was convicted of a shooting rampage that left three men dead and eighteen children fatherless.

Vettere had lived in Meaderville with the Joseph Ciccarelli family a few years prior to the shooting. Ciccarelli, however, took Vettere to court for taking liberties with one of the younger Ciccarelli daughters, and the judge ordered Vettere to post bond or leave Butte. Having no money, Vettere went to Basin where he worked in the Jib Mine. Acquaintances said that he spent most of his spare time shooting targets. On November 22, 1925, Vettere returned to Butte and ambushed Ciccarelli and his friend Antone Favaro, killing Ciccarelli instantly and mortally wounding Favaro. Vettere then fled the scene. In his haste to leave the neighborhood, he encountered John Deranja, a night watchman on his way home from work, and shot him dead, too. Police theorized that Vettere mistook Deranja for a policeman. Vettere was eventually convicted only of the Favaro murder because the dying man named him as his killer.

On the day of the execution, Vettere went berserk in the jail as officers tried to take him from his cell to the scaffold. Screeching like a fiend, he attacked deputies with a pipe ripped from

the shower room and a knife made from a spoon. In an effort
to subdue him, deputies filled the entire cellblock full of tear
gas, subjecting themselves and the other prisoners to its effects.
Deputies finally overwhelmed Vettere, strapped his arms and legs,
and dragged him into the jail yard where the scaffold awaited. As
Vettere struggled, he swore venomous oaths, promising to return
for vengeance even as deputies put the noose in place and ended
his miserable existence.

Another well-publicized execution took place on May 18,
1906, when Miles Fuller was hanged for the grisly murder of
Henry Gallahan. The two old-time prospectors had long been
sworn enemies. Fuller claimed that Gallahan had laced his flour
with powdered glass and his sugar with strychnine, but witnesses
testified that it was the other way around. The longstanding
quarrel, according to Fuller, had begun when he stopped Gallahan from molesting a child. But Fuller was a hermit with a
surly disposition, always armed with a wicked-looking knife, and
locals were afraid of him. Gallahan had been shot in the head
and his throat slashed from ear to ear. Authorities found the gro-
tesque remains in a brickyard near the McKinley School. Fuller
never admitted guilt.

The scaffold that awaited Fuller had already served its
gruesome purpose at least four times in Butte and twice when
on loan to Powell County. The "galloping gallows"—so-called
because it traveled on loan—was the type constructed without a
trap into which the condemned fell. Rather, the method was to
loose a 350-pound weight, jerking the unfortunate victim into
the air. The dismal frame, painted black, was assembled in the
jail yard. A member of the sheriff's force well-versed in the black
art of strangulation prepared the regulation hangman's rope,
ordered from Chicago, and tied the noose with the required nine
wraps and proper knot.

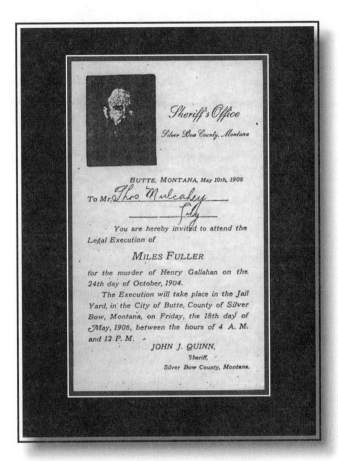

Invitation to the hanging of Miles Fuller. Butte Miner,
October 17, 1909.

Fuller was a pitiful figure, elderly, feeble, and frightened.
He went to the gallows wearing his old, tattered hat, while a large
crowd, some having scaled walls and climbed rooftops, tried to
get a view. Only those with invitations, however, were allowed
inside the yard. Fuller's death was the fastest recorded in Montana, taking only two minutes from the jailhouse door to the end.
Pallbearers to carry the coffin to the waiting wagon were difficult
to find among those present, most being superstitious about per-

forming such a task for a condemned man. Finally two ministers, two city officials, and two newspaper reporters volunteered. The day was rather gray, but the weather was not particularly inclement. However, as they carried the casket to the waiting wagon, a tremendous, unexpected clap of thunder broke the silence; it was the only one of the morning. Some believed it to be a portent.

A few years later Deputy Sheriff Tom Mulcahy, who had been present at Fuller's hanging, experienced a series of weird occurrences. Mulcahy had in his possession some relics from Fuller's hanging that included an invitation to the event, a piece of the hood placed over the condemned man's head, and a piece of the hangman's rope. Mulcahy and others believed that the ghost of Fuller was attracted to the relics, and especially to a photograph included on the invitation to the hanging. Many times Mulcahy reportedly saw the ghostly form come through the window of his lodging room on the ground floor of the jail. The window looked out on the courtyard, not thirty feet from the site of the scaffold. The apparition moved, in a kind of foggy, dim light, from the window to the bureau and sometimes even opened the drawer. When Mulcahy turned on the light, it would vanish out the window. After numerous such incidents, Mulcahy took the scrapbook containing the relics and put it under his pillow. He settled back to sleep, but immediately felt something tugging at the scrapbook.

Mulcahy's roommate had a similar experience. The unnamed roommate was about to fall asleep when something grabbed his neck. What felt like a piece of cloth and a rope dangled over his face. At that time, the roommate did not know about the relics Mulcahy had in the drawer. The men were quite shaken, and Mulcahy offered his bed to anyone who would stay there to try to disprove what had happened. No one would volunteer.

The jail yard was also the scene of weird sightings. The janitor reported a man moving about in the shadows in the exact place where the scaffold had been. The yard was locked and an immediate search revealed nothing. Others also believed that they saw the tortured spirit of Miles Fuller, and though unfamiliar with him, described him exactly as he appeared on his trip to the scaffold.

A strange coincidence centered on another deputy, Mike Friel, who lost his job soon after the visitations in Mulcahy's room began. Friel had sometimes shared the room and had also seen the ghost. He got into some trouble that the *Butte Miner* declined to explain, although according to Deputy Mulcahy, it was a silly affair very uncharacteristic of such an upstanding, well-liked young man. A week after he lost his job, Friel was duck hunting at the foot of Montana Street. He inexplicably stepped in front of his cousin's shotgun and died some seventeen hours later of a wound to the shoulder. Deputy Mulcahy claimed that Friel was always a very careful hunter, and that he could not imagine why Friel would step in front of a gun in such a manner. There was talk that Miles Fuller put the hoodoo on Mike Friel.

As these incidents were unfolding, the present Butte–Silver Bow County Courthouse was under construction. The courthouse jail and yard that were on the site in 1909 were being torn down in stages and replaced. As the new facilities replaced the old, the incidents—at least reports of them—stopped.

The new gallows that served for the hanging of Anthony Vettere had been constructed for the triple hanging of Sherman Powell, Frank Fisher, and John O'Neill on January 14, 1918. Fisher and O'Neill shot miner Thomas Higgins as he came upon them robbing a man on South Wyoming Street. Although wounds to Higgins' foot and leg were not serious, he died of blood poisoning a month later. Many believed that the crime was not a capital offense. Powell, a Great Northern employee, fatally stabbed a co-worker who cheated him in a card game during an overnight stopover at Butte. Powell was very well-liked and even left thank you notes for his jailers. All three men hoped Governor Sam Stewart would hear their appeals, but denial came only hours before their executions. Butte building contractor Michael D. O'Connell built this state-of-the-art gallows so that it could be disassembled in seconds and stored or shipped. It stood above a concrete pit ten feet deep and sixteen feet square. The condemned stood on the crack where two hinged doors joined. At the touch of a lever, the doors opened and the men fell, theoretically breaking their necks so they would not strangle. Powell fainted before the executioner pulled the lever, and the other two had to wait several minutes while deputies revived him. Next to die on the new gallows were Monte Harris and William Harris. These men, who were not related, were convicted of killing a hotel desk clerk during a robbery. They died together on this gallows in 1923. Vettere was its final victim.

The present courthouse, completed in 1910, occupies the same site as the original one and has its quirks, claim several generations of courthouse employees. The elevator has elicited the strongest reactions. According to the building's janitors, it can only run when someone inside the car pushes the buttons. But when the building is dark and the halls are empty, up and down it goes, stopping on one floor and then another, opening its doors for nonexistent passengers from the top floor all the way down to the basement.

In the basement, stored to this day in the dark recesses of the stately hall of justice, is a disassembled gallows. Which gallows it may be, the first or the second, is open to question. Either way, the shadowy figure that roams the courthouse halls could have been an unfortunate victim of either instrument.

Montana Standard staff writer Peter Chapin discussed the courthouse ghost in an article on October 31, 1991. The ghost, described by those who have seen him, is six feet tall, wearing cavalry boots and a wide-brimmed hat that hides his features. The night watchman claimed to have seen him many times, roaming through offices and halls. Others claim to have seen a headless miner. Neither description fits Miles Fuller, whose beard was a distinctive feature mentioned in the descriptions of the 1909 spook. And the shadowy figure seems not to be so familiar with the present-day courthouse. It is said that he follows an unusual path, walking into walls. A Butte architect observed that he seems to walk through walls following the floorplan of the old courthouse, not the present building. Whoever this ghost might be, according to Chapin, it is a spook you can believe in. ✸

Mansion Mysteries

BUTTE HAS SOME OF THE MOST BEAUTIFUL Victorian-era homes in Montana. Towers, turrets, exquisite stained glass, inviting wrap-around porches, and bay windows symbolize the wealth and prestige of its early citizens, many of whom worked for copper king William Andrews Clark. The homes along the streets in Butte's more elite historic neighborhoods, tucked against the hillside, are reminiscent of San Francisco's lovely "painted ladies." These charming homes stand in marked contrast to the legendary place that was the black heart of Montana. The mines ran shifts twenty-four hours a day; the saloons and the women of the red-light district likewise served their clientele round the clock. Sulfuric smoke poisoned the air and soot was so thick that laundry hung on backyard clotheslines was dirty long before it dried. Hardly a blade of grass poked above the soil. Today, homes are landscaped, and in the summer months, the lawns are green.

Butte's west side retains a good share of the state's most beautiful Victorian-era homes. Professional men, prominent businessmen, and copper king employees brought their families to live in this exclusive neighborhood in the Mining City, where fortunes were tied to the success or failure of the industry beneath the streets. Two elegant houses in particular have had disquieting pasts. One of these lovely historic homes, built circa 1900, is distinguished by a wreath motif above the porch entry and an impressive octagonal tower. It was originally home to George Forsythe, manager of Clark's Columbia Gardens. The lavish amusement park was the copper king's gift to the people of Butte, and it became their pride and joy. Forsythe's home reflects the affluence accorded him in his prestigious position. By 1913, the residence was home to a prominent Butte couple. The husband retired from the food industry in 1952 and died in 1964. With her husband gone, the widow remained at home but suffered poor health. According to local gossip, she was something of a recluse and seldom left the second floor of her house, where she passed away in 1969.

The house changed hands three times during the 1970s. In 1979, Deb Corak had a friend who lived in this home. Deb is sensitive to the energies of places and claims a number of psychic experiences. The friend was aware of Deb's gift and asked for her help. Things did not seem right in the house, and the lady's two children were having difficulty sleeping. They were terrified of something but they were unable to articulate their fears. Deb agreed to pay a visit.

Several decades later, Deb still vividly recalls the details. She entered the home and toured the first floor. The house had a pleasant feel to it, nothing sinister or disturbing. The interior was lovely, beautifully and tastefully finished by skilled craftsmen, and well maintained by its owners. Deb pronounced the first floor friendly and welcoming. They started up the stairway to the second floor. Once on the landing, Deb stopped abruptly. "It starts right here," she said to her friend.

Deb could feel the negative energy. She explained that sometimes spirits are place-bound and cannot move, but this particular spirit had a certain mobility. The unpleasant feeling flowed throughout the upstairs, in the main bedroom, and in the sitting room where the children slept. There was, however, one tiny bedroom that the unpleasantness did not touch. Deb asked her friend about this particular place. She replied that it had originally been a storage closet that was recently converted to a small sleeping room. It was not a place that a person would frequent and so might logically escape human imprint. The worst, however, was the bathroom, where the negative feeling was nearly overpowering. When Deb remarked about this, her friend paled.

She informed Deb that the longtime resident had died there.

Although research reveals that the elderly woman had raised several children and been active in a local youth organization, Deb got the strong impression that this second-story spirit did not like children, and did not want them around disturbing her quiet and messing up her rooms. Deb told her friend as much. As they started downstairs, they paused on the landing and again Deb remarked that she had the distinct feeling that they were not alone.

"They say that the lady who died upstairs never left the second floor," said the resident.

"Oh yes, she did," said Deb. "She is right here on the landing. She comes here often to gaze out the window."

Deb's friend soon decided that the upstairs layout was "inconvenient" and moved with her children out of the house.

Deb had an experience in another Butte home where she lived for a time some twenty years ago. It, too, was a beautiful old house, distinguished by a round turret with a conical roof. Deb had no knowledge of its history or who might have lived there, and she loved the house, except for one thing. There was an upstairs walk-in closet that had a very disagreeable ambience. "Sometimes," says Deb, "it took everything I had to open the door." She had visions of a little boy locked in the closet as punishment, and this incident—fraught with terrible suffering and awful fear—left a dreadful imprint. It was not a place where someone had died, but the residual energy of this child's horrible experience was palpable.

One evening Deb hosted a small party. Eight friends gathered around the kitchen table, talking. The conversation turned to the house and one guest spoke up, "What's with that upstairs hallway?" The person described experiencing negative "vibes" in the area. The dreaded closet was just on the other side of the wall. Deb decided to ask each guest in turn to think about the house and decide what place was the most uncomfortable. She went around the table. Every single person zeroed in on the same area, pinpointing either the closet itself or an area, like the hallway, that adjoined it.

Some time later, Deb moved out and put the house on the market. She was not terribly surprised one day when the realtor called her to say that potential buyers had also been disturbed by something in the house. The realtor wanted to let Deb know that an exorcism was being performed even as they spoke.

While the documented history of this house reveals no such child abuse, that kind of information rarely was recorded. However, there is an interesting coincidence. H. Lowndes Maury, a Butte attorney, built the home circa 1906. Maury was a well-respected city attorney who was a passionate socialist and protector of the underdog. He often defended clients in opposition to the powerful Anaconda Copper Mining Company. Maury and his wife raised their seven children in the home, and while they sometimes struggled to make ends meet, they were devoted parents. Maury himself was accomplished in many areas and was a champion chess player. And something else: Maury had "the gift." Lowndes Maury's daughter, Lydia Lowndes Maury Skeels, writes about her father and his accomplishments in *One American Family: Some Maury Memories, Legends and Records.* She relates how her father was reputed to be psychic because of two incidents known to family and friends. The first had to do with a longtime friend and patron, Frank Corbett, a member of the Montana legislature from Butte who died in 1901. Maury was in a Helena hotel lobby and saw his friend across the room. The last time they had met, he and Maury quarreled over Corbett's heavy drinking and parted in anger. Many witnessed Maury stride across the lobby, offer his hand and exclaim, "Frank, I'm sorry for the other day, and I'm mighty glad to see you and say so." Unbeknownst to Maury, Frank Corbett had recently died. No one else in the lobby had seen his ghost.

The second incident occurred in the 1910s on a snowy December night in the Maury house in Butte. Lydia's birth was imminent. Maury was alone in the living room when he heard a horse approaching the house. He heard the rider dismount, unsaddle the horse, throw the saddle to the ground, and slap the animal to send it to the stable. Maury ran to fling open the door just as the nurse attending Mrs. Maury upstairs came down the steps on her way to the kitchen. As she stood behind him, it was obvious that he addressed a visitor that only he could see. "Confound it, Harry Maury. Get out of here and never come near me again," Maury bellowed. Lydia's birth followed after this event. The child was born with a cowl over her head. According to an old wives' tale, this was a sign of psychic ability.

Lydia heard the story years later from the nurse who had attended her birth. Maury then reiterated how Harry, the family ghost, had appeared to him at the house that night in Butte. Harry, dressed in his Confederate Army officer's coat, had bothered other family members in the past. Maury himself had encountered the ghost several times as a teenager, as had his uncle and his grandfather. After his tirade at the doorway, Harry did not bother Maury again.

The closet in the Maury house, although unexplained by documented evidence, could have several logical explanations. The Maury household was a haven for newly arrived immigrants, and the family frequently took them in, offering temporary employment. Perhaps one of these displaced women employed in the household had a child who the mother felt needed this kind of harsh discipline. Another possibility is that the event with the closet occurred after the Maurys sold the home in 1954. Several other families owned the home before Deb's occupancy in the 1970s. Perhaps the incident occurred in these later decades.

It is an interesting happenstance that this residence was home to two such gifted occupants. Whatever the reason for the closet trauma, Deb Corak was surely not mistaken about its negative energy. Further research could uncover the cause, but for the time being Deb is confident in what she sensed. "You know how you can be walking down the street and you feel someone watching you from a window? I feel these things," she says, "off the back of my neck." ✸

A Discordant Note

IN ANOTHER BEAUTIFUL BUTTE MANSION that needs to remain anonymous, a group of friends had the fright of their lives. The thought of this incident even today is enough to prickle the spine. They were spending a pleasant evening chatting at the dining room table when an odd noise silenced them. Listening intently, they heard it again: a strange moaning sound. It started out low, hardly discernible, gathered strength, then ended abruptly. Again came the low-pitched moan. It hung in the air, growing like a scream, building momentum from some deep place within the house. They knew it was coming from the third floor, and that someone would have to go upstairs to find the source of the terrible moaning.

The thought of going up those stairs filled them all with dread. They mutually agreed that they would go in a group. As they ascended the grand staircase, one step at a time, the sound rose and fell like a ghastly, ghoulish greeting in a low-budget horror movie. The anticipation of reaching that awful sound was compounded by a general uneasiness about the third floor. There, the house creaked and the ballroom, in its fading splendor, evoked memories of times past and beautiful people long since dead.

They reached the third floor and the moaning had risen to a deafening, all-encompassing crescendo. It was loud; it was eerie; and it left eight adults holding hands and wishing for the comfort of their own homes. Then the monstrous groaning sigh ebbed and died, producing a silence equally disturbing, but rose again immediately with renewed vigor. They flung open the door and peered into the dreaded inner sanctum of the ballroom, eyes adjusting to the dark. They all stopped at once and stared. Against one wall stood a pipe organ. Outside, the wind was blowing and it whistled into the ballroom through a small broken pane of stained glass. The realization began to dawn. The wind's target was a bass pipe and the death rattle moan was only the rise and fall of the wind hitting a low note! ✺

The Ghostly Madam at the Dumas Hotel

THE DUMAS HOTEL IN BUTTE makes a lasting impression on visitors. To step across its threshold is to experience layers of history in the most literal sense. The main floor, once a tasteful series of parlors separated by heavy paneled pocket doors, offers glimpses of its Victorian past in the peeling red flocked wallpaper and fancy embossed plaster walls. In contrast, bright red-orange woodwork and 1960s orange shag carpet jar the senses, fitting the stereotype of a mid-twentieth-century whorehouse, which it was. Through many decades, the women of the Dumas plied their trade with the miners and businessmen of Butte. After hours, they enjoyed the camaraderie that comes from shared experience. Sometimes in the quiet, the working girls' phantom laughter resounds throughout the three floors.

The spacious second-floor rooms, each with a numbered transom and a corner sink, recall the glittering 1890s when copper kings had money to burn and parties were unending. The rooms were bright with silk and velvet; beautifully clad women entertained their gentlemen guests, and Chinese servants carried elegant trays of exotic food and drink.

The upstairs and the basement reveal a shocking disparity. Down the dim, dank stairway the anticipation builds and the visitor feels something akin to panic. Once in the shabby, dimly-lit basement hallway, colors fade to gray. Here the lowest women in the red-light hierarchy serviced miners around the clock. They worked in shabby rooms while ten-minute timers measured out a dollar a minute for their efforts. It is a depressing place, but somehow compelling, poignant, and eerie all at the same time. The air down there is stale, unpleasantly cold, and makes your skin crawl. You can't help but wonder what comes out of the shadows at night with the lights off and the building empty. Transomed doors and windows arranged

Ten-minute timer and other artifacts in a basement crib at the Dumas Hotel.
Courtesy the author.

like those upstairs frame the narrow hall, but here they recall lonely
spider-webbed portals to damp underground crypts.

At the back of the Dumas on the first floor, a padlocked door
leads to a darker passageway flanked by two more transomed crib
doors. The end of this passageway opens onto a brick-paved street
once known as Pleasant Alley, where hundreds of one-room back-
street cribs housed the heart of Butte's tenderloin. On paydays, cash
stuffed in trouser pockets, four thousand miners strolled the board
sidewalks looking for a good time. The women obliged, and some
of them made a good living. Pleasant Alley was, however, a dangerous place. The working women of Butte called their neighborhood
the burnt district, its tiny cribs, by the hundreds, as useless for any
other purpose as burned out shells. Violent encounters were all
too common. Thieves, drug addicts, aging whores, and embittered

johns (called "secretaries" in Butte) lurked around every corner. The bricks of Pleasant Alley, later known as Venus Alley, witnessed stabbings, beatings, and shootings. When the cribs in Venus Alley and those in the basement of the Dumas closed for good in 1943, the alley festered. Later madams at the Dumas called the brick-lined labyrinth of empty cribs Piss Alley. The cribs and the once-fancy parlor houses with their faded trappings of long-ago prosperity fell victim to arson and urban renewal. Their dark history lives mostly in local legends. The Dumas alone remains intact, a social archive with nearly a century of human memories imbedded in its walls.

The Dumas Hotel is a place of secrets. An active brothel from 1890 to 1982, it has a tangible feel and personality that are more easily imagined than described. For its last fifty years of operation, women at the Dumas have taken care of each other, shared gossip, good times and tears, unaware of the grim history beneath their feet. The basement cribs of the Dumas, in use from the turn of the century to 1943, lay untouched like time capsules until the early 1990s, when building owner Rudy Giecek rediscovered them. The Dumas has yielded up some of its treasures to him, and history bears out some of the stories that its walls have to tell. There are personal letters, money, pictures, postcards, and personal items tucked in nooks and crannies. A crawlspace under the floor, concealed behind a dresser, offered a hiding place during raids, while a refrigerator with air holes drilled in the back served a like purpose. Chewing gum painted over in the doorjambs and window corners tells another story, and one small basement crib has a penciled list of debts incorrectly tallied. Giecek came across an antique evening bag stuffed into a hollowed-out space in a wall. Inside the bag was a small tin box. Inside the box, carefully wrapped in a bit of silk, was the bright yellow body of a long-dead canary.

There are other things, however, about the Dumas that are not so tangible. Giecek, who has operated an antique mall,

"Hidey-hole" in a crib at the Dumas Hotel. Courtesy the author.

brothel museum, and old-time photography studio in the building, calls the Dumas a very scary place at night. Those who have spent a night there say that ghosts wander about in its forty-three rooms, moving in the shadows and disturbing the dark. They lurk in the hidden recesses of the building, glide through the dingy basement cribs, and float up the stairs. They show themselves on occasion, or draw attention in other ways.

Over the decades a number of madams occupied the roomy front apartment on the second floor. These several lovely rooms have spectacular light that streams into the high-ceilinged spaces from tall bay windows. Elinor Knott lived in the madam's apartment while she ran the Dumas from 1950 to 1955. One cold night in February, so the story goes, Elinor was about to embark upon a new life. She was tired of her women and their complaints, of the rude customers, and especially tired of Butte. She had packed her belongings in her suitcase and was ready to go. Her lover had promised to leave his wife and come for her. They would leave the dingy mining city to start a new life together, a *respectable* life.

Elinor's lover never came for her that night. The next morning at 11:20 Bonita Farren, a supposed friend of Elinor's, found her body. She sent for the doctor, who pronounced the forty-two-year-old woman dead of natural causes. He estimated that she had been gone for about an hour. Dark whispers among acquaintances suggest that she committed suicide by mixing alcohol and sleeping pills. There was no inquest.

Bonita Farren immediately succeeded Elinor as madam at the Dumas. She and her husband, John, moved into the second-floor apartment. Perhaps Bonita had worked for Elinor, and perhaps they really were friends. But perhaps they were not. At any rate, John Farren died in 1964 and Bonita died of cancer in her room at the Dumas in 1971. Ruby Garrett then took over as the last madam. On October 3, 1981, there was a brutal robbery. Mrs. Garrett was pistol-whipped and robbed of a substantial amount of money. An employee's boyfriend had committed the crime. Although he was apprehended and sent to prison, the well-publicized incident led to a federal investigation into the business at the Dumas. The IRS convicted Mrs. Garrett of tax evasion, and the Dumas closed in 1982. Rudy Giecek acquired the building from Ruby Garrett in the early 1990s. Because of the condition of the building, legal problems, and a lack of funds, the Dumas is today in a precarious position, its preservation in jeopardy.

Under Ruby Garrett and after, various people have reported sighting a spectral woman with a suitcase in the Dumas. One account came from an employee who worked there in the 1970s and returned to the Dumas on a visit to Butte. She told Giecek of her experience staying in the building alone one night. She was sitting in the bathroom upstairs at the end of the hall, with the door open. She had a view of the hallway and the corner stairway that leads to the main level. As she sat there, she saw a woman carrying a suitcase walk past the door and descend the stairs. She was so shocked she didn't move until the top of the woman's head disappeared down the stairs. She hurried down the stairs after her, but the woman was gone. Although she thoroughly searched the building, the front and back doors were locked and barred shut. No one could have gotten in or out that quickly.

A Missoula psychic who recently visited the Dumas believes that the woman with the suitcase is Elinor Knott. But there is more to the story. The psychic received the distinct impression that Elinor did not commit suicide but was murdered. She had packed her suitcase and was ready to leave, and some- one did come for her. Who it might have been is a mystery, and how the cause of death went unreported is also unexplained. The psychic, however, believed that Elinor was betrayed by her lover, suffered violent trauma to her back, and died as a result. Elinore's spirit moves throughout the Dumas, reliving the violent act. This information confirms what Rudy Giecek has always maintained: that Elinor Knott did not die of natural causes. According to the official record, she was destitute when she died. But Giecek says Elinor's friends claimed that she possessed a red Cadillac, a brand new Harley Davidson motorcycle, jewelry, and plenty of money at the time of her death. None of these was found.

Teri Goodson of San Francisco has made several trips to the Dumas and has even spent a night there, sleeping in Giecek's photography studio. She, however, was not afraid. While she does not describe herself as psychic, she does believe she can identify at least three entities in the building, and that they have communicated with her. She is sure that one entity is Elinor Knott. Teri can sense the trauma that ended her life, but she believes that Elinor stays around the Dumas because she is worried about its preservation, and wants to make sure that nothing happens to it.

A second entity Teri has encountered is a man named "John." This may be a play on words, or it may be his real name. One client did expire in an upstairs room (the parish priest was called to administer last rights in the doorway, the man being too large for the women to move), but his name is unknown. Perhaps the spirit is John Farren. Whoever it is, Teri feels that he likes to be around the old-time photography studio on the first floor, but that that he and Elinor, who knew each other in life, roam freely throughout the building.

The third distinct spirit is that of Bonita Farren. Teri senses that Bonita is a tortured soul in need of help. Teri has prayed with her and offered her comfort. Before she died, Bonita felt that she had been cheated out of what was rightfully hers in business dealings and thus carried this anger to the grave. Bonita's ghost is not always friendly, and Teri says that she does things to get Rudy's attention, especially in the basement. Rudy has indeed taken a number of strange photographs down there with unexplained images in them.

A few years ago, a visiting artist needed a place to work. Rudy allowed her the use of the madam's apartment on the second floor. The ample windows and bright daylight were ideal for painting. The artist set to work, but each time she faced the canvas,

Artist's portrait of the ghostly madam at the Dumas Hotel. Photograph by author (1997), used with the permission of Rudy Giecek.

she felt a strange compulsion to paint the face of someone she had never met. Over and over she painted the same face. *It haunted her.* Canvas after canvas went in the trash until finally she gave up and went elsewhere to paint. Rudy rescued one of the portraits from the garbage. The woman is fortyish, wearing a hat with a medium brim and a hint of a coy smile. Bonita Farren? Elinor Knott? She smiles because only she knows the answer to the question.

As long as the Dumas stands on Mercury Street, its ghosts will roam the forty-three rooms. Upstairs, downstairs, along the hallways, and in the pockets of darkness they wait and watch. They are at home there—the old ones whose energy grows faint, and the younger ones who sometimes show themselves in unexpected ways. They wait in the dark, keeping vigil, keeping their secrets. ✸

A Midnight Visitor

THE BACK YARDS OF HOMES IN BUTTE'S EARLY SUBURBS once ended in mine shafts. Southeast Butte was such a place; today it is rather like a forlorn stepchild of a once-mighty parent. On East 2nd Street stands a house where a large family filled its rooms for the better part of half a century. This house is a simple Queen Anne-style worker's cottage, like ones found all over Butte, where miners and laborers lived with their families, working hard as the years rolled by, looking forward to the day when the house would be paid off and the children grown. There is nothing glamorous, nothing romantic about it. Research tells us that the longtime owner was a blacksmith for the Anaconda Copper Mining Company for nearly fifty years, and at least for the last forty of them, he owned this cottage. He and his wife raised six children in the house, and records indicate that all grew to adulthood. Perhaps extended family, even boarders, lived with the owners, as was the practice in Butte during the copper mining boom. Research, however, has failed to confirm the secret that this house seems to harbor.

Mark Reavis, Butte-Silver Bow's longtime historic preservation officer, once owned the house on 2nd Street. Mark is a level-headed architect, in tune with Butte's heritage and well aware of the town's historic significance as the labor capital of the world, the "Gibraltar of Unionism." Red-haired, lanky, and genuine, Mark is also a skeptic, and even though he has experienced something he cannot explain, he has no use for the supernatural. His story is told here with his permission on the condition the reader be cautioned that, despite this experience, he still does not believe in ghosts.

In the early 1980s when Mark first came to Butte, he and his wife bought the aforementioned house. As Mark is an architect with a love for history, the couple immediately set about putting the house back together the way it was originally built, restoring the rooms one by one and furnishing them with items that would have been typical in a miner's home of the Victorian era. It was never a fancy house, nor did they furnish it that way. Rather, they strived to bring back the period ambience that once gave it personality. Mark even went so far as to install a bathroom "Side arm" water heater just like the one that would have originally provided its turn-of-the-century residents with the luxury of a hot bath.

One night after the work on the house had been nearly finished, the couple was sound asleep and the family cat lay curled peacefully at the foot of the bed. Mark awoke suddenly. He later recalled that his first thought was that he was dreaming. Through the open door, he had a clear view of the dimly lit hallway that led to the bathroom. Darkness blanketed the bedroom, and as he blinked against it wondering why he was in this strange dream-like state, something at the end of the hall caught his eye. He felt an unreasonable fear beginning in the pit of his stomach, its icy fingers creeping along his spine. As he lay motionless, blinking in the darkness, unsure of the source of his fear, he saw it again: a subtle movement down the hall.

"Oh, come on. I'm only dreaming," he thought to himself. But the cold terror did not go away, and he felt his eyes straining to convince himself that he hadn't really seen anything. But there it was again, moving down the hall toward the bedroom, as quiet as a cloud, subtle as mountain fog that settles over alpine meadows. "Mist," thought Mark. "How weird. What is mist doing in my house?" The vague, misty swirl of wan light came closer. Slowly, slowly it moved down the hall toward the bedroom door. As it reached the doorway, the mist began to assume a more definite shape, *a distinctly female shape*, but small, like that of a child. The shape's image grew ever sharper—like twisting the lens on a camera to get it in focus—until he saw a little girl of ten or eleven standing at the foot of his bed. Mark's fear paralyzed him, and he could only stare. He felt a scream building deep within his chest, but before it could rise to the surface, the cat bolted straight up into the air from the foot of the bed. With a terrifying wail, the frightened animal arched its back, puffed its tail, and in a flying leap landed at Mark's throat, drawing blood. The terrified cat then urinated on his pillow. The shape instantly disintegrated and the cat tried to calm down, furiously licking his coat. Mark woke his wife to tell her about his experience, but she put her hand up to silence him, saying, "It's not real—go to sleep." Mark slept; his wife could not.

The next morning when Mark awoke, he discovered angry scratches on his throat and began to realize that perhaps the apparition had not been a dream. When he mentioned it to his wife, she admitted that she had seen it, too.

The apparition never presented itself again, but some time later an odd thing happened. One sunny afternoon, Mark was working in his yard. He heard a noise and looked up to find an old gentleman shuffling around outside the house, peering in the windows.

"Can I help you, sir?" Mark asked the uninvited visitor.

"Oh, I'm sorry if I startled you. I was just looking around. I grew up in this house, and I was just curious to see how the years had treated it." The old gentleman seemed harmless enough.

"Would you like to come in and see for yourself?" Mark asked, always eager to show his handiwork to an interested guest. And it occurred to him, as he thought about it, that maybe the old man could answer some questions about the home's original appearance which he had painstakingly tried to restore.

The two stepped over the threshold and the old man let out a sigh. "Oh," said he. "Oh, my. This is just like it was when my mother kept house here. We had a sofa right there like you

—

do. And we had a table there. Just so!" He scrutinized the room, and then commented, "This is just like stepping back in time. Just like I was a boy again."

The pair made their way to the bedroom, and the visitor peered in. "Yes. Yes. Yes, indeedy. Just like my parents had it. The bed was there, and the cradle—there was always a baby—was right there exactly as you have it."

They walked down the hall to the bathroom, and the old man said, "Why, I don't believe it. We had a water heater tank just like that. Right where you have it! Looks just the same." The old man grew thoughtful then, and his eyes clouded a little.

"I had five brothers and sisters that grew up in this house. We were a noisy family, all crowded in here. One sister, though, had something wrong with her. She wasn't quite right. She was, as I guess you would say today, developmentally challenged. My mother had to watch her all the time. One day, though, she fell in the bathroom. Fell right into that heater. She had horrible burns all over. She died a few days later."

Mark felt himself begin to tremble. He was afraid to ask this question, but he had to know. "How old was she?" he asked, but he already knew the answer.

"Why," said the old man, "I reckon she was ten or eleven when she died." ✸

Helena Tailings

Mule train on Helena's Main Street, 1870s. Montana Historical Society Photograph Archives, Helena.

John Denn

GROCER JOHN DENN HAD JUST CRAWLED into bed and was about to wind his pocket watch when he heard a rap at the back door. He turned back the bedclothes, put on his carpet slippers, and answered the knock in his nightshirt and drawers. It was not unusual for Denn to receive customers he knew after hours at his back door. The patron wanted a bottle of whiskey, so Denn took up a candle, a funnel, and a bottle and went down to the cellar to draw it from the cask. As he bent down to open the spigot, the intruder hit him once on the top of the head with a hammer-like weapon, punching a fatal hole in his skull. As Denn fell to the floor, the murderer dealt two more terrible blows—one above each eye. Denn lay in the cellar for some hours in a puddle of gore. Customers made the grisly discovery the following morning, October 28, 1879, when he failed to open his store. During the investigation of the crime scene, passersby on the street could see through the cellar windows the body of John Denn prostrate before the liquor barrel, his face frozen in a bitter smile.

Denn had kept large sums of cash in his business and talked too much about it. His neighbor, John Shober, wandering through the crime scene while police searched the premises, found nearly $7,000 missed by the intruder hidden in a tin box in the cellar. The safe, though, was empty and its key was never found. Despite a $12,000 reward, no one was ever charged with the crime. Folks whispered about their neighbors and speculated about who knew more than they were willing to tell. And in the aftermath of John Denn's death, frightened citizens made the first documented use of the well-known Vigilante warning, "3-7-77."

Nearly ten years later, longtime Helena photographer Mrs. Mary Ann Eckert made a shocking confession just before she died on May 3, 1888. She claimed to have gone to Denn's house, roused him on the pretext of wanting a bottle of liquor, lured him to the cellar where she took a hatchet and, in her words, "hit him a lick." Some believed the confession; others did not. Denn was not killed with a hatchet. But everyone agreed that Mrs. Eckert had been peculiar and eccentric. Friends described her as "possessed of vague forebodings," and she often told them that she was under great mental torture. She was obsessed with the Denn murder. The deputy U.S. Marshall told reporters that Mrs. Eckert had repeatedly come to his house late at night to accuse John Shober of killing Denn and of also trying to kill her. Mrs. Eckert had, in fact, herself been "hit a lick" over the head with a hatchet by an unknown person a few years before. Could Shober have committed that act of violence? Mrs. Eckert had some quarrel with Shober, and she confessed to her nurse that she had tried to pin the crime on him. John Shober's name is scattered throughout the sensational confession. Even though it had been he who found the moneybox at the crime scene, he was never interviewed—as far as the record goes anyway—by the authorities.

An acquaintance reported that a year before her death, he had chanced to meet Mrs. Eckert near the site of Denn's murder. Workmen were excavating for a new building where Denn's store had stood, and the former cellar was exposed. Mrs. Eckert looked "pale and ghastly, her hair disheveled," and she seemed greatly troubled. He asked her what she was doing up so early. Mrs. Eckert was slow to reply, but finally turned her eyes toward the cellar and pointed at it. In an unnerving voice she said, "I am watching that accursed spot."

Mrs. Eckert had come to Helena in the early days of the mining camp and had operated a photographic studio since 1868. It was she who took the famous grisly photograph of the double hanging of Wilson and Compton in Helena in 1870. She had always maintained her business and her residence in the worst

Madame Mary Ann Eckert photograph of the hanging of Joseph Wilson and Arthur Compton on the Hangman's Tree in Helena, April 30, 1870. Montana Historical Society Photograph Archives, Helena.

part of town, earning her an unsavory reputation. Gossip suggested that Mrs. Eckert began her Helena career as a hurdy-gurdy dancer; that she had a long-standing romantic liaison with a prominent and very jealous Helena man; and that she had swindled the husband with whom she came to Montana. Mrs. Eckert had charged him with abandonment and asked the court to waive fees because she was too poor to pay. Yet she and her daughter went to Paris soon after so that her daughter could take art lessons. The courts never finalized the divorce. Even so, Mrs. Eckert passed herself off as a widow, but in her will she named John S.

Eckert, her husband, as a beneficiary. She left him one dollar.

Mary Ann Eckert owned $25,000 worth of Helena property, a substantial sum of money back then, and much of it was red-light real estate. At the time of her death she had plenty of money, but she had only one debt: an overdue loan for $630 owed to John Shober. This very prominent attorney, a respected member of the Helena community and the prestigious Montana Club, figures repeatedly in the mystery. Shober, Denn, and Mrs. Eckert had all known each other since mining camp days. Denn frequently loaned money to the women of the red-light district, including in years past to Mary Ann Eckert. Both Shober and Denn were bachelors. Could there have been more than money involved, and could one of the men have been jealous? Two weeks after Denn's death the newspaper reported that John Shober had gone to Bozeman on business, and that his many friends had noticed that he was "looking more like himself than he had in years." What did that mean, and why would the paper publish such a strange remark if there were not already some suspicions about him? Something clearly was not right about this case. Most people finally concluded that Mrs. Eckert's confession was made to screen someone guiltier than she was herself, but everyone agreed she had shared in the blood money.

After Mrs. Eckert's confession was made public, the newspaper reported a new oddity in the case. A man came to a Helena attorney's office claiming that his business partner had murdered Denn. The man had a wild, haunted look and seemed to be suffering from a heavy mental burden. He said that he had gone to bed exhausted and was suddenly awakened by an icy breath that sent a chill down his spine. He sat up with a start and at the end of his bed, standing there natural as life, with the three great holes in his forehead, was John Denn. The spirit in a piteous, pleading tone exclaimed, "You know the murderer. Hand him over to justice that I may sleep in peace." Slowly the phantom faded.

By the time the attorney notified the authorities, the accused business partner had fled. The frightened snitch was later judged insane and sent to an asylum, and the murder remained unsolved. For many years after, Helenans dreamed of the restless ghost of John Denn, whose cellar today lies somewhere just east of the grassy stretch between the Lewis and Clark Library and the old Federal Building. Some say that when the harvest moon is full and pale and October nights are waning, the lonely ghost of John Denn roams the grassy slope where Wood Street used to be. With three great holes in his head and a bitter smile upon his face, he searches for the murderer that only he can identify. ❀

The Ghosts That Weren't

THE OLD CATHOLIC CEMETERY ON OAKES STREET where John
Denn was laid to an uneasy rest no longer exists. Today the new
St. Mary's Catholic Church north of the Capital Hill Mall marks
one former boundary. Homes and lawns border the other sides.
Robinson Park, named in honor of the only neighbor opposed to
the park's creation in the 1970s, is a green haven in the middle of
suburbia. The park was once the center of the old burying grounds
where, between the late 1860s and the 1920s, more than seventeen
hundred souls were interred. The earliest burial records for the
Catholic Cemetery on Oakes reveal that many were the victims of
the dangers that plagued all mining camps—diphtheria, meningi-
tis, childbirth, accidents, and consumption. Among the infamous
characters that still lie buried in the former cemetery are Helena's
well-known madam, Chicago Joe Hensley, and five convicted
murderers executed by hanging. When the area was subdivided for
residential development, relatives claimed the remains of some two
hundred individuals and moved them to the newer Resurrection
Cemetery on Montana Avenue and other locations. Unclaimed
tombstones lie dumped in a pile on the outskirts of Helena, but the
bodies they marked remain. Workers laying power lines in the cem-
etery-turned-suburbia had orders to leave remains undisturbed, but
the hundreds of graves left below the sod caused no small difficulty.
Montana Power Company maps, according to one employee, show
where the lines make neat ninety-degree detours around coffins
throughout the neighborhood.

Before this delicate rearrangement of the dead, though, the
graveyard haunted local children. It seems to be a universal law
among youngsters that one does not tarry in a graveyard without
paying the consequences. This was especially true for kids in the
Sixth Ward, who knew that *this* graveyard was a place where

spirits were rumored to be especially restless. The young toughs growing up on the south side of the tracks devised a rite of passage, likely passed down from brother to brother and father to son, which tested a boy's courage. The feat was to steal into the Catholic Cemetery in the pale of the moon, light a fire among the tombstones, and piss it out. How many generations of young Helenans accomplished this daring act is a matter of speculation, but it was a deed that kept many a schoolboy from a good night's sleep in fearful anticipation of his own turn.

The late Einar Larson, whose father had an early-day meat market down along the railroad tracks by the depot, related a tale about a terrible fright his cousin Melvin had in the cemetery late one night in the early 1920s. Whether or not Melvin had attempted the rite of passage is unknown, but the young man had an experience that likely proved more frightening than any boys' game. And the historical record bears out the central facts that Larson recalled.

The sun had long set. Melvin was on his way home, and he was tired. Cutting through the cemetery was a much shorter way to his family home in the Sixth Ward, so he decided to take the shortcut even though the thought of stepping over some long-dead pioneer filled Melvin with dread. The old cemetery was a creepy place. The air was cold, and Melvin could see his breath escaping in white cloud-like puffs as he hurried along. The chill moonlight painted the tombstones dismal shades of gray, illuminating with pale light the final resting places of hundreds of early-day residents. As Melvin dodged headstones in his path, he shivered at the thought of the bones that lay beneath his footsteps, and imagined a cold hand reaching up to prevent him from attaining the warmth of his mother's kitchen. By the time he reached the midway point through the graveyard, a patchy fog had covered the moon. He tried with difficulty to choose the quickest path between the sunken depressions marking the oldest untended graves and their tombstones, some tilted askew and others completely fallen over. At the edge of the graveyard, Melvin emerged from the swirling mist and surprised himself with a long sigh. He had been holding his breath for the last few steps and only the sight of the wooden fence marking the boundary of the burial grounds made him realize it. He would have to scale the fence, and then he would be safe and almost home.

Melvin saw something move on the other side of the fence. It was not a trick of the moonlight, since globed streetlights illuminated the roadway beyond the fence. Melvin could see down Oakes Street to the intersection with Livingston. A sign to the side of the unpaved juncture warned where the tracks of the Great Northern Railway crossed Oakes Street. Melvin stood quite still, breathing hard, and peered across the graves along the cemetery's edge. Then he saw it again. To his horror a figure in white materialized before his eyes.

He felt a cold wind brush his cheek. The leaves rustled as the motion of the breeze skittered through the graveyard and reached the spectral figure, making the white robe flutter as the apparition seemed to glide along the road. A peaked hood or cowl covered what would have been its head if, thought Melvin, the thing had a head. As he squinted from his vantage point just inside the graveyard's edge, the boy was now grateful for the darkness that enveloped him as he crouched silently behind a headstone. As he watched, frozen by fear, a second figure and then a third emerged from the other side of the road. Melvin bit his knuckles to stifle a cry and concentrated on counting. Four, five, six, seven, eight figures finally moved in a straight line. Their ghastly faces—or so Melvin imagined—were shrouded in the folds of the weirdly pointed cowls. The robes looked like something an Arthurian wizard might have worn. He watched the figures glide along, one by one, until each reached the corner and literally disappeared into the ground. As the last pointed head melted into the earth, Melvin got his footing and hightailed it toward the fence, falling over tombstones, skinning his knees and elbows. He leapt over the fence, fell again in the dirt roadway but was hardly mindful of the gravel embedded in his bloody knees. He finally reached his house and burst in the back door, white as a sheet and blubbering some incoherent tale about ghosts in the old cemetery. As his mother dressed his wounds, his family teased him unmercifully. Melvin didn't care. He was just glad to be home, safe and sound.

The next morning the newspaper reported that the Ku Klux Klan—esteemed at least by some in Montana for its charitable acts during the depressed 1910s and 1920s—had been in town to bestow a large donation on the Oakes Street Methodist Episcopal Church. This church happened to be located just outside the Catholic Cemetery. The ghosts Melvin had seen were only the Klansmen, dressed in their white flowing robes and pointed hats, descending the stairs to a basement meeting room. ✺

Mamie's Bells

A FEW YEARS AGO THE CITY OF HELENA INSTALLED a wrought-iron fence around the parking lot of the Lewis and Clark Library. The daughter of longtime Helena resident Alma Pauly Everett donated the fence to the city. A small plaque explains that the fence once graced the home of wealthy Thomas Cruse, a man who left his imprint all over the community. He donated a quarter of a million dollars toward the building of the St. Helena Cathedral; his name is on an urban renewal cut-through, Cruse Avenue; and an ostentatious mausoleum in Resurrection Cemetery bears his name. Cruse also bought and carried the bonds that eventually built Montana's Capitol Building. The legendary wealth and star-crossed life of Thomas Cruse thus had a far-reaching impact on the Helena community. The short text of the plaque only hints that there is more to the story.

Thomas Cruse, affectionately called "Tommy" by those who knew him, was a stubborn Irishman who came to Helena in 1867, so impoverished and down on his luck that he spent that first night on the street huddled under a blanket. Despite the ridicule of other miners who urged him to give up, years went by while Cruse sought his pot of gold. He staked his claim west of Helena. From the tiny opening of his mine he crawled down to the workings day after day, hiring no one to help for fear of being robbed of his undiscovered fortune, and taking time off only to venture into Helena for supplies. After long years of backbreaking labor on hands and knees, Cruse began to take significant gold ore out of his Drum Lummon Mine. Later, with borrowed capital, he established Lewis and Clark County's first amalgamated silver stamp mill at the town he named Marysville in 1878. Less than a decade later, Cruse was a rich and well-respected man.

On a sparkling snow-covered March morning in 1886, the

crusty fifty-year-old Cruse wed twenty-five-year-old Margaret Carter, sister of future U.S. Senator Thomas H. Carter. Some thought the union a little strange, but Carter was Cruse's legal advisor so it was, in that respect, a convenient match. Helena had never before seen such a celebration. A large crowd of spectators moved toward the Cathedral of the Sacred Hearts on Helena's Catholic Hill to the merry chime of sleigh bells. The bride wore a gown of cream silk trimmed in Spanish lace with a court train and lace overdress; the maid of honor was elegantly attired in cream Albatross cloth trimmed in ruby velvet. Cruse sported a "black diagonal" with Prince Albert coat, white gloves, and tie. The scent of orange blossoms and other exotic blooms, bought from local florists' stock and shipped from as far away as Portland and St. Paul, perfumed the frosty air. Champagne, claret, port, and wine punch flowed freely at the reception in the separate men's and ladies' parlors at the Cosmopolitan Hotel. When the buffet was served, tables groaned under a dazzling cornucopia of turkey, chicken, quail, and other meats as well as elaborate cakes, ices, and myriad delectable desserts. A huge crowd of well-wishers partied far into the night, with drinks in every saloon all over town compliments of Tommy Cruse. There was so much revelry and so many drunken incidents that Helena women vigorously, but temporarily, renewed an interest in the temperance crusade in the months that followed.

On New Year's Eve, just ten months later in the same cathedral, candles surrounded the black-velvet-draped casket of Thomas Cruse's bride. Mrs. Cruse had reportedly been of nervous temperament, and following the birth of a daughter December 15, she succumbed to "nervous prostration" while the town buzzed with whispered speculation. Was Cruse disappointed not to have a son? Was he truly mourning the loss of his wife? No one knew for sure.

The child, Mary Margaret, was nicknamed "Mamie" and was such a jewel to her father that he fairly smothered her. His vast wealth caused him concern that she might be kidnapped. Thus, Mamie led a very sheltered life behind the iron fence of her father's mansion at 328 Benton Avenue. Daily she would accompany him in his fine carriage to the Cruse Savings Bank and amuse herself under his desk. Every evening he would take his Mamie to the Montana Club where, for a little dance on the bar, Mamie would be treated to a tiny nip of creme de menthe. This would later prove an unfortunate choice of indulgence for the golden-haired child.

No doubt Mamie was spoiled; she possessed everything her heart desired—except the freedom of other children. She was stubborn and strong-willed like her father, even as a very young child. Mamie scandalized children even younger than she by playing in the aisles and making noise during Sunday Mass, a serious transgression discussed around many a Helena dinner table. When Mamie was seventeen, she eluded her father and ran away with her sweetheart. The couple got as far as Elliston before Cruse caught up with them and made the grave mistake of fetching her home, setting in motion another phase of the tragedy to come. Helenan Lester Loble knew Mamie and her father. He wrote that "this delightful and beautiful little girl grew to womanhood dreaming of life beyond the iron fence." After the interrupted elopement, Mamie was sent away to school and into a world that was not always kind to her.

At twenty, Mamie married Wall Street broker Alvar O'Brien. The marriage ended soon after in divorce. A second marriage in 1911 to Harry Cotter went unrecognized by Cruse, whose Catholicism did not permit divorce. He persisted in reminding Mamie that she was "living in sin." Mamie was estranged from Cotter when the police plucked her from a road-

Mamie Cruse, circa 1900. Montana Historical Society
Photograph Archives, Helena.

house on the outskirts of Butte and returned her to Helena in the
autumn of 1913. The town whispered and wondered if her father
knew what kind of life his Mamie led. Her father acknowledged
Mamie's addiction to alcohol, but nothing more. Speculation was
that Mamie was also addicted to drugs, or perhaps afflicted with a
venereal disease, or perhaps both. Amidst rumor and scandal, suffering from an undisclosed illness, Mamie was placed into the care
of the sisters at the House of the Good Shepherd. It was a telling
choice since the sisters' mission was to protect and rehabilitate
wayward girls and young women who wished to reform. People

wondered if it was Mamie or her father who wanted her there. The sisters returned her to her father's house on Benton Avenue a few days before she died on the Tuesday before Thanksgiving, 1913. Bright's disease was listed as the official cause of death.

Helena, then, not only mourned the loss of Cruse's child, but also seemed to sense the end of an era, realizing that this tragic event might signal the end of Thomas Cruse and his benevolent patronage. Mamie's obituary carried little about her short life. Instead, it contained a lengthy account of her father's contributions and profuse appreciation for his "devotedness to the community's advancement."

The following spring Mamie's estranged husband, Harry Cotter, brought a lawsuit against Cruse, challenging her will. Witnesses in the ensuing courtroom drama included Bishop Carroll and the mother superior of the House of the Good Shepherd. In the course of the scathing trial, Mamie's name was "blackened and besmirched." Lester Loble recalled seeing Cruse during this time sitting on the steps of his mansion, dejected and lonely.

Thomas Cruse caught a bad cold and died on December 20, 1914, very rich and very unhappy. His beloved cathedral was dedicated five days later on Christmas Day, and his was the first funeral in the magnificent cathedral that he had helped build. But before he died, Thomas Cruse gave Helena one last gift. In the nearly–finished cathedral, fifteen bronze bells were added to one of the twin spires. Each is inscribed: "In memory of Mary Margaret Cruse, by her father, Thomas." The bells that still ring out over the town on special occasions were once known as "Mamie's Bells."

For many more years the twenty-two-room mansion presided over its prestigious corner at Benton Avenue and Lawrence Street. The home had been built in the early 1880s as the residence of T.C. Power. Cruse purchased it because he believed the Irish superstition that it would be bad luck to live in a home that he built for himself. The grand residence had five Italian tile fire-places and floors of cherry and mahogany. In 1963, the house was torn down to make room for a modern apartment building.

The fence that today stretches part way around the library's parking lot was rescued from demolition. It is a strange coincidence that the fence wound up there. Although Thomas Cruse was an uncanny businessman and founder of a highly successful bank, he had no use for education, refused to donate toward the building of Carroll College, and purportedly never learned to read.

Thomas Cruse, his wife Margaret, Mamie, and other family members were laid to rest in the showy mausoleum in Resurrection Cemetery. Unlike most family crypts that bear the surname only, this one is inscribed "Thomas Cruse." It can be clearly seen from the interstate that runs along the eastern outskirts of town. In an unusual arrangement, all the other graves in the cemetery—nuns, priests, and prominent Helenans—form a circle around the mausoleum. Even the graves of such powerful men as Senator T.C. Power, Senator Thomas Walsh, and businessman Peter Larson (who also donated substantially toward the building of the St. Helena Cathedral) face the Thomas Cruse tomb.

Residents of the neighborhood north of the cemetery grounds and motorists passing by have remarked over the years that when the night is especially dark, they have noticed *some-thing* white moving about in the cemetery. The faintly glowing *something* catches the eye as it floats near the Cruse mausoleum. Sometimes it roams among the headstones of the neatly mani-cured grounds. One resident claims the cemetery caretaker told her that whoever it is makes frequent appearances. Surely the restless spirit is Mamie, dressed in white as she often did, and as lost in death as she was in life.

Preeminent Montana historian Dr. Richard Roeder, a character in his own right, wanted to write about "Mamie's

Cruse Mausoleum. Katie Baumler, photographer (2001).

Bells." On several occasions he remarked that he thought the story important to the history of the community and wanted it remembered. He had not written the article when he passed away just a few days before Christmas in 1995. His colleagues mourned his death, but it was a shock when his obituary appeared in the *Independent Record* on Christmas Eve, 1995. Directly next to Dr. Roeder's photo was an article by reporter Grant Sasak recounting the entire story of Mamie's Bells. ✸

Little Girl Lost

Anna and William Zastrow built the attractive house that sits on 9th Avenue in 1887 or 1888. Anna died in 1904 and William remarried the following year. When he died in 1912, his second wife, Marie, kept the home until 1927. The Zastrows had no children, but like most of their neighbors they took in boarders during the 1890s and thus their rooms were always occupied. Who these boarders might have been is not a matter of record, but some tragedy left its stamp in the house. A former homeowner related her experience in the house, and historian Jon Axline adapted part of the tale as a Halloween story for the Helena *Independent Record* in 1995. This is the rest of the story.

The property owner in the early 1970s had a daughter of two or three. The little girl's neighborhood friend was a couple of years older, and he would come to play upstairs in the house. The children rode their tricycles endlessly around the upstairs hallway that formed a three-sided square around the stairwell. It was safe enough, enclosed by a sturdy railing. From one side, down the hall, across and down the other side, and back again they would pedal as fast as their little legs could go. She could hear them laughing and squealing and pedaling like mad as she went through her chores downstairs.

One morning she heard them and thought to herself how nice it was that her daughter had a playmate that lived close enough that he could come and go. She hadn't heard him come in, but when the laughter began upstairs, she felt reassured that the children were entertaining themselves. As lunchtime approached, she headed upstairs to get the children ready—calling them never seemed to work. The childish laughter ceased as she moved up the stairs, but she heard voices whispering. When she reached the top, there was her little daughter playing quietly by herself. There was no sign of the neighbor boy and no other child upstairs, but at the head of the stairs an empty rocking chair rocked slowly back and forth.

Not too long after this incident, she awakened in the middle of the night to the sound of a child's crying. She leapt out of bed and in a few steps stood at her daughter's door, but the little girl was sound asleep. A few nights later she again dreamed she heard sobbing. Fighting her way from the depths of a deep sleep, she awoke to realize that she wasn't dreaming. The sobbing was real. But this time as she turned over in bed she saw the child standing there at her bedside. The little girl was clad in a dark Victorian-era dress and her brown hair hung in long ringlets. The old-fashioned curls fell around her face, hiding her features. She stood there for a long time crying as if her heart would break. Then the apparition quietly faded.

If the homeowner had any question that her mind was playing tricks on her, or that she was having some weird dream, the reappearance of the same image over the next several months dispelled her doubts. The young mother became so depressed over the poor child's extreme sadness that she could think of little else during the day, but she did not know what to do about it.

After several of these sightings, two other apparitions joined the little girl. The child stood by the bedside crying, but this time she turned, walked out of the room, and there at the top of the stairs a man and woman waited, visible through the open bedroom door. The woman wore a black silk dress of Victorian vintage. The man, clad in a black and white checked suit, sported a black mustache. Each took a hand with the little girl between them. It seemed as if the child did not want them to take her. Her cries became louder, and she tugged as if to free herself. The woman's skirts were so full that on afterthought, the living observer felt a keen and poignant empathy for the child. The billowing skirts pressed around the sobbing child must have been suffocating. As the three held hands, they walked through a wall and disappeared.

After this incident, crying in the night still awakened the homeowner, but though the child sometimes sobbed at the bed-side, more often the little girl would move out to the hall and gaze out across the valley. Always, the ringlets fell across her face, obscuring her features.

These visitations frightened the homeowner but worse was the sadness emanating from this little girl. Her lingering misery cast the mother into a severe depression. She wanted to help this child. Instinctively she believed that the child had lost her parents and did not know how to find them again.

After the sale of the house, and as moving day neared, a circle of friends gathered in the backyard one summer evening. They held hands and thought pleasant thoughts and tried to communicate with the sad little girl. They tried to tell her that all was right if she would only take that step into the next world. The small ceremony did not help, and still the nighttime crying per-sisted. Then after a second attempt, the crying abruptly ceased.

Carolyn Cunningham, who has lived in the house since 1972, attests to the fact that a childish spirit may still occasionally visit. Two disconcerting events convince her that she sometimes shares her home with an uninvited guest. When Carolyn moved into the house on 9th Avenue, a treasured possession was a Stutt-garter clock she bought in Germany that had always worked perfectly. As soon as she brought it into her new home, the clock stopped. She took it to be repaired, but the watchmaker could find nothing wrong. It worked perfectly in his shop. She took it back a second time, but again it worked just fine in the shop. As soon as she got it home and hung it on the wall, it stopped again. She finally gave the clock to a friend, and in the friend's home it kept perfect time.

Equally as baffling was a chair Carolyn had reupholstered that seemed to have its own inner life. She was excited to have the finished chair back after a long time in the shop. The upholsterer delivered it to the house late one evening. She took off the protective plastic and stood back to admire how well the fabric complemented the style of the chair. Then she saw it. To her horror a huge blotch of purple spread in an ugly ring across one side of the chair's lower back. She thought to herself in a panic, "Did I do that?" Then she calmed down enough to think about it. She couldn't have been responsible for the stain since she had just taken the wrapping off. "The upholsterer must have done it, or it happened in the shop, but if I accuse him he will surely deny that it was his fault," she reasoned. Carolyn decided that she would have to wait until morning and would then try a chemical stain remover. She had spent a tidy sum on this chair and was afraid that it was an unredeemable disaster. She gave up and went to bed. The next morning Carolyn went to look at the chair. She could not believe what she saw. The purple stain was completely gone. It was as if it had never been there at all.

Carolyn can't explain the clock or the disappearing stain. Although she did not know about the previous owner's experience with the crying child until recently, she had reached her own conclusions about an unseen prankster. The child seems to have come to terms with her tragedy. She just returns occasionally to play her little tricks. To this day neighbors sometimes notice that when the upstairs windows are heavily iced over in winter, the hallway window has a peculiar oval in the center that is clear of frost, just the size of a child's face. At least one neighbor has seen the small face of a little girl in the oval, gazing towards the valley, her features hidden by her long brown ringlets. ❂

Count Your Blessings

ANNABELLE AND HER LATE HUSBAND, RON, LIVED in a beautiful Victorian-era home in the Lenox Addition on Helena's east side, where the couple raised their three children—Kent, Brent, and Lisa. From the 1970s to the early 1990s while she lived in the house, Annabelle savored its period ambience. The home was built circa 1889 for William D. Wheeler, gold assayer in charge of Helena's U.S. Assay Office. Wheeler lived in the home until the late 1890s. The position of assayer, obtained by presidential appointment, brought with it social prestige and required frequent entertaining. Important guests including politicians, businessmen, and dignitaries enjoyed Wheeler's lavish hospitality. Ladies in sweeping gowns and elaborately trimmed hats and gentlemen in cutaways attended garden parties and teas on the gracious wraparound porch.

In many respects the Wheelers and Annabelle and Ron Richards were much alike. Ron began his career as executive assistant to Senator Lee Metcalf, then served as executive assistant to Montana governors Forrest Anderson and Tom Judge, and was later director of the Department of Highways (now Montana Department of Transportation). Like Wheeler's political appointment as assayer, Ron's employment was also dependent upon politics, and required the couple to entertain frequently. Annabelle hosted beautiful teas, receptions, dinner parties, and social events. It almost seemed like the 1890s again with the house full of guests and animated conversation. The vintage home seemed to like the attention and the new life that Annabelle and Ron brought into its spacious rooms.

Annabelle always felt that the house was special. She and the house shared a special bond, and she had some unique experiences while she lived there that deepened her attachment to it.

She came to accept the fact that she shared her home with several different spirits who always seemed to visit her in the wee hours of the morning. The first encounter came when Annabelle was in bed awake but with her eyes closed. She had the strong feeling that someone was standing at her bedside looking down at her. She had the definite impression that it was a woman wearing a Victorian-era dress and a large picture hat. The feminine presence seemed to linger in the house, and Annabelle was quite aware of her, although the spirit never actually revealed herself.

One early morning Annabelle was again lying in bed awake with her eyes shut. She had a feeling that something or someone came into the room. She thought at first it was "Gov," the family's big collie–Australian shepherd. She opened her eyes and didn't see anyone in the room, but the feeling persisted. She had the strong and distinct impression that it was a child. On several other occasions, she awoke with the feeling that this same little child had crept into bed with her, cuddling spoonlike next to her as young children do. Annabelle never felt the least bit of fear, but rather found the experience pleasantly endearing. Once, she distinctly felt someone sit down on the bed beside her, but when she opened her eyes, no one was there. Still, she never felt frightened.

Another early morning experience, however, shook her complacency about nocturnal visitors. She felt a presence enter the room, but this time Annabelle sensed that it was a boy of ten or eleven. He was mischievous, even *impish*, and not so nice. A pillow pressed down over her face. She gasped, afraid she couldn't breathe, and just as suddenly, the mischievous "imp" was gone. Only in retrospect did Annabelle feel some trepidation after this strange encounter.

The third-floor attic was once the servants' quarters. Tiny little gaslights, still in place but no longer functioning, dotted the walls. These were the only amenities the servants of long ago enjoyed. Their comfort in winter depended upon what little warmth rose from vents in the floor. There was also a wonderful third-floor turret. Kent, Brent, and Lisa loved to sleep in the quaint round room with its three little low-arched windows. They put their beds by the windows where they could lie down and look out over the Helena valley. They could see what was going on for miles. One warm day Brent was spending some quiet time alone, lying in bed in the tower room, looking out the window. Across the room was a small alcove that served as a closet, although it did not have a door. Samantha, the family's little black cat, was enjoying the view with Brent when suddenly she stiffened, arched her back and stared across the room at something near the alcove. Samantha's eyes were unblinking, fixed on something Brent couldn't see. Her eyes grew so huge and she stared so hard that Brent became frightened and raced out of the room. As he moved past the alcove area Samantha had been staring at, he encountered a distinct cold spot. He could think of no explanation for the strange frigid air on a warm day.

The children were teenagers when Annabelle had her most unsettling experience in the house. It was about six in the morning and still very dark, but it was that fleeting moment just between darkness and the break of dawn. Annabelle slept in a second-story bedroom with the head of her bed against the wall next to the doorway that opened onto the landing. She was half awake when she heard two sets of footsteps on the stairs. Instantly awake, she listened intently. She heard two men whispering in the quiet as they came up the stairway. As they neared her door, she distinctly heard one of them whisper, "Are you all right?" The other man answered with a mumbled, "Yeah." The two men had been speaking just on the other side of the wall. She froze, realizing that they were only inches away. She thought that one man was at the door, and the other had somehow come into the room and moved behind her bed. With a shiver she realized he was moving toward her. She jumped out of bed and ran out of the room.

Soon after this incident, Annabelle and Ron moved temporarily to Washington DC, where Ron was executive assistant to Senator John Melcher. They were gone for six years, from 1983 to 1989. In the interim, several sets of tenants rented the house. Kent was married by this time, and he, his wife DeLyn, and Lisa were living in the house. One night DeLyn and some friends were downstairs while Lisa lay in bed upstairs. They began to hear heavy footsteps impatiently pacing the floor overhead. At first they all thought it was Lisa, but when DeLyn went up to check, she found Lisa fast asleep. The footsteps were so ominous and insistent that they checked again, but Lisa was still sound asleep. They became very frightened and called the police. Kent arrived, meeting the officers at the door, and as they came in the house, they all heard the footsteps. The officers drew their guns and climbed the stairs, but found no one.

The next tenant was an acquaintance that Ron had met through his association with the Grandstreet Theatre. Ron and Annabelle trusted him to take good care of the house, but apparently the house didn't take to him. After a short time he informed Ron on the phone that he couldn't deal with the music. Often when he was upstairs, the radio downstairs would inexplicably turn on by itself. One of its favorite tunes was "Easter Parade." The young man's roommate heard the music, too. They moved out.

Other tenants also felt a presence in the house. Annabelle later wondered if the spirits were unhappy in her absence and didn't like other people living in the house. She wondered if, perhaps, the little imp now sought new victims, or if the men on the stairs had returned. Whoever or whatever spirits they were, they misbehaved and badly frightened the tenants. When Ron and Annabelle returned to their Helena home, Annabelle immediately knew that something had changed in the house. It was not the same. After making some inquiries, the tenants informed her that they had become very frightened from their own experiences and had called their Protestant clergyman. He and several others performed an exorcism. The group had gone through every room in the house to rid it of the troublesome spirits. Annabelle was devastated to find that the ceremony had worked and that her house was utterly empty. While it was still a lovely home, it no longer had that unique ambience that Annabelle had so admired. Although Ron never had any of these experiences, Annabelle missed the occasional visits from whomever it was that she had come to know. To this day it upsets her to think that this drastic step was taken without her knowledge or consent. ❁

The Haunted Cabin

HELENA'S PIONEER CABIN AT THE FOOT OF REEDER'S ALLEY and the intimate little neighborhood that clusters around it have a long, fascinating, even mysterious, history. The cabin was one of many little houses built by the first miners who followed the gold rush to Last Chance Gulch in 1864. This area was Helena's first neighborhood. Today the cabin is the oldest standing building in Helena with a documented history, and the Reeder's Alley neighborhood, dating to territorial days, is the oldest intact piece of the community. And it has stories to tell!

Among the first miners to stake claims along the little stream called Last Chance was a handsome black-bearded bachelor who built a one-room dwelling. There he spent the winter of 1864-65 snug in his little cabin. With the spring, his brother joined him, bringing a wife and three young daughters. They built another cabin in front of the first one, and there the two brothers mined the claim. The gold camp bustled with miners and merchants in the mid-1860s. Within a short time loud music and rowdy miners soon proved the gold camp was no place to rear three young girls, and so the family moved on. Other miners and their families came and stayed for a time before they followed other opportunities or moved into more comfortable homes as Helena grew.

Above the row of cabins, Louis Reeder, a Pennsylvania brick mason, began to buy lots in the 1870s. He added onto the small buildings he purchased and built others, using the rowhouse style he had grown accustomed to back east. His little brick apartments, an eclectic mix of brick, stone, and wood, offered miners a better place to live than hastily-built, uncomfortable cabins like those below the alley. Reeder's Alley was first home to the miners whose claims lay along the gulch or in the nearby hills. When the gold dwindled and mining ended, one-time miners who turned to other livelihoods continued to call the little apartments home. A few of the quaint little cabins at the foot of the alley north along Park Street sat abandoned and neglected; others were taken over by Chinese residents who cultivated the little valley to the east, growing fresh vegetables they sold to the community. New residents tore down some of the earliest cabins, and uninhabited ones began to decay. By 1885, the area was considered the "bad" part of town, and the little miner's cabins still standing along Park Street became home to gamblers, prostitutes, and the Chinese community.

In the summer of 1885 the local newspaper reported a haunted shanty on Park Street, near the fringe of Chinatown and the string of red-light dwellings that had once been home to miners. It might have been the Pioneer Cabin itself, or what is today the Caretaker's House, or a nearby cabin. Policemen on their nightly rounds had heard terrible moans coming from this cabin. Nearby residents had complained of bloodcurdling screams and awful thudding and whacking sounds of men fighting. Other neighbors reported seeing a haggard old woman peering out of the window. The cabin had certainly developed a bad reputation. According to a local legend, it had once been home to a snaggle-toothed old hag who tricked several miners out of their gold dust and then murdered them to keep them quiet. The story goes that she found the 3-7-77 Vigilante warning tacked to her door and fled the gulch.

The fact that the sinister commotion came from inside the derelict old place, once home to miners who had come to a bad end, disturbed the residents of Reeder's Alley. They felt a kinship with the old hag's supposed victims, and they wanted the disturbances to stop. One night several policemen on their rounds again heard the pitiful moans and groans with their own ears.

They broke into the cabin, splintering the wooden door, and all the while the dreadful sounds surrounded them. They stood there in the pitch darkness, fumbling for a match. The sounds of heavy breathing seemed to press down on them, and the deep moans curdled their blood. One of the men finally found a match and struck it. The sounds stopped abruptly. Emptiness greeted them in the bright circle of light.

As the years stretched into decades the alley's scary reputation stemming from the haunted cabin stuck. Legends grew about the people who lived and died in the neighborhood. Reeder's Alley served as a carriage path for young girls from the west side that attended St. Vincent's Academy on Catholic Hill. Their parents told them not to tarry on their way to and from school, and not to travel through there unaccompanied.

In 1897 when the great gold rush to Last Chance Gulch was passing into memory, streetcar driver Bob Murray cut through Reeder's Alley on his way home for dinner. There had been a recent rainstorm, and he caught a glint of something in the gutter. He picked up a gold nugget the size of a pebble. Soon half the nearby Chinese community was panning for gold right there in the alley, and resident caretaker James Gorman had all he could do to keep them from starting up new diggings. The alley yielded up no more gold, but the Helena *Herald* speculated that the nugget washed down from Mount Helena to let residents know that "there is plenty of gold up there if they will only go seek for it." The only question as to the truth of this story is that it appeared in the paper on April Fool's Day.

Into the 1930s and 1940s mostly single male pensioners and a few faded, aged ladies of the evening continued to live at Reeder's Alley. One ex-miner with consumption (a common occupational hazard known as the "miner's con") hooked his toe to the trigger of a shotgun in his tiny apartment and blew his brains out.

The last resident of the Pioneer Cabin was George Mitchell who moved into the old, ramshackle place in about 1903. Mitchell lived there until his death in 1933, operating a wood and coal business and selling chickens and eggs from his backyard. Mitchell died intestate with no known relatives, so his property went to the city. He had not been a good housekeeper, and the place was a mess. When workmen went in to do repairs, they found that Mitchell had stuffed gold and silver coins in the floors and walls. Dollar bills were stuffed in bags, old socks, and wrapped in receipts dating back twenty years. Mitchell never spent anything, stashing his earnings in every conceivable hiding place all over his property. City workers eventually recovered several thousand dollars. Maybe some of it is still there.

George Mitchell (seated in the wagon) with the Pioneer Cabin, right and the Caretaker's Cabin, left, circa 1904. Montana Historical Society Photograph Archives, Helena.

History has thus endowed the Pioneer Cabin and the surrounding neighborhood with a certain mystery. Jan Sinamon, who lives next door in the Caretaker's House and gives the Pioneer Cabin tours, had an eerie experience that adds to its mysterious character. She has lived in the neighborhood for nearly twenty years, and she and her late husband, Don, together were longtime caretakers of the cabin. On an ordinary morning in November of 1989, the day after the state's centennial celebration, Don died quite suddenly. It was about 7:00 in the morning, and Jan suffered shock and had an emotionally trying time of it.

Later in the morning, Jan was walking between her house and the Pioneer Cabin. She noticed that the cabin's side door was wide open. It was off-season, and she had not been in the cabin at all for a few days. The door had been locked and the alarm system was hooked up and functioning. Yet, the door stood wide open, the motion sensing alarm still set and untriggered. Jan went to shut the door and despite repeated efforts, could not make it close. The door no longer seemed to fit in the doorway. She got her neighbor to come and help, and together they forced the door shut and locked it again. Such a thing had never happened before, and has not happened since. It seemed as if Jan's husband, who loved the Pioneer Cabin and knew as much about it as anyone, was insisting that she be watchful. Jan believes it was his way of making sure that she would continue to take good care of it. And this she has certainly done.

Hundreds of children and adults have gone in and out the cabin's back door over the years. On a day not too long ago after a number of children had visited, one youngster had gone out the back door and returned with something in his hand. He showed her what he had found at the back door, lying in plain sight in the dirt. Jan was astonished at what the youngster held out for her to see: a very large, very old, and very worn marble. ✸

The Mumblers

A ROW OF QUAINT VICTORIAN-ERA HOMES ON UNPAVED 10th Avenue in Helena is a charming reminder of the capital's formative years. These homes were originally exactly alike, built around 1890, and are unusual in that they are quite narrow and tall. For such small homes, these are especially charming inside because of their high ceilings. Built at the same time as the nearby St. Helena's Catholic Church on Hoback Street, they housed for at least twenty years European immigrant families, including many from France. About ten years ago, one of these picturesque houses was home to Tom Quinn, his wife Julie, and their two small sons. Tom is not one to believe in the supernatural, but he can't explain the events his family experienced while living there.

Tom had lived in the house with his family for several months when one night he was downstairs watching TV. Everyone else had long been asleep, and some late-night program had Tom's attention. During a lull in the drone of the television show, Tom became aware of voices. It wasn't that he had never heard these voices before, but the sound had always been so subtle and low that he had ignored it. Like the droning of bees in a hidden nest that you can ignore until one stings you, he didn't pay much attention to them. In an epiphany, the muttering voices in the dead quiet late at night in his home struck him as unusual. Whoever the mumblers were, the voices were all masculine, and they seemed to be having a good time. Tom could not distinguish words, only the amicable tone. The murmuring voices sounded to Tom as if they were engaged in a card game, shut in some unseen room inside the house. Try as he might, Tom could not find the source of the mumblers, and as long as he lived in the house, he was aware of their droning, but he put it aside.

While the family was moving out and Julie packed boxes,

she heard the mumblers for the first time. "I couldn't make out what was being said," Julie remembered, "but it was very loud. At first I thought I was hearing voices in my head, until I asked our five-year-old if he was hearing them, too. He told me he was. I looked around the house and outside and found no one." Julie then called Tom at work to ask him if he had ever heard the voices. He confessed that he had been hearing them for a long time. In the following days as the family packed their belongings, the agitated mumblers grew ever louder. The card players seemed to have lost their good cheer, and the Quinns were very glad to finally lock the door behind them for the last time.

The 10th Avenue house voices, though, proved less troublesome to the Quinns than the spirits that seemed to haunt their boys. They were having difficulty toilet training their two young children because both were very much afraid of the bathroom. The boys insisted that there was a man in there. They said that he was all in black shadows; the blackness swirled around him like a robe except that his face was always visible. This, the boys claimed, was easy to identify. When Tom questioned them about who they thought it might be, the children always replied with sincerity that the man looked just like "the man on the quarter." The Quinns thought this reference to the image of George Washington so very odd that they could hardly imagine their small sons made the story up, but they could think of no other explanation.

Several years later, Dennis Homer, a co-worker of Tom's, happened to mention that before they were married, his wife Christina lived in the house on 10th Avenue just after the Quinns moved out. Dennis and Tom began to compare notes. Dennis, a confirmed skeptic, admitted that he had heard the voices, too, but he heard them when he was outside in the backyard. Once, one of the voices was so insistent that Dennis turned around and asked an empty yard, "What did you say?" Christina heard the mumblers, too. She, like the Quinns, always heard them when she was inside the house. They agreed that the mumblers were *inside*, and Christina felt they were somehow centered in a closet in which there was a trapdoor that led to the cellar.

Christina always thought the house had a weird feeling, and when her father came for a visit, he thought so too. She was especially disturbed by a closet door in one of the two upstairs bedrooms that had a slide bolt on the outside. It bothered her because the door shut and latched perfectly, and hardly needed to be locked in such a way. She never liked to open the door because it made her wonder who, or *what*, she might let out when she opened it. Then there was a French door downstairs she deliberately shut and latched before going to bed; on more occasions than she cared to remember, it would be open in the morning. And finally, in talking with her next-door neighbor, Christina learned that the house had a reputation for being haunted that long preceded the Quinns' residency.

In searching for a thread that might tie all these loose ends together, a very eerie coincidence came to light. Montana pioneer Mary Ronan wrote about Helena in the 1860s and 1870s. Among Mary's descriptions of the early-day Helena community is a discussion of the Catholic priests she knew and greatly admired. Among them was Father Leopold Van Gorp, S.J., a widely respected priest in Helena in the early days. Father Van Gorp was from Belgium, and his native language was French. By the 1890s, he was the business manager at St. Ignatius Mission, but he often came to Helena. Father Van Gorp's advice was much sought after on all kinds of business matters among both parishioners and non-Catholics in Helena. It is possible that Father Van Gorp might have visited this French-speaking neighborhood on occasion, perhaps counseling the residents on financial matters, and even joining in a friendly card game. His presence among the immigrants made a great, even indelible, impression upon them. Most intriguing, however, is Montana pioneer Mary Ronan's casual description of this well-loved priest. She said that he was a man of splendid physique, handsome in the long black robe that swirled around him. And more than that, according to Mary, many remarked about his striking resemblance to George Washington. ❀

Reverend Leopold Van Gorp, S. J. L. B. Palladino, S. J., Indian and White in the Northwest *(Baltimore, 1894).*Montana Historical Society Photograph Archives, Helena.

Lady of the House

FOOTSTEPS THAT ECHO IN AN EMPTY BUILDING, a name softly whispered when no one else is there, the feeling that someone is watching from the shadows, a fleeting rush of cold air, and other unexplained occurrences like these are not so unusual at Grandstreet Theatre. The supernatural events are well enough known for it to have been cited in *Haunted Places: The National Directory*. This outstanding Helena landmark harbors a poignant history, making it all the more worthy of its reputation.

Some of the eerie events at Grandstreet are likely connected to Clara Bicknell Hodgin, a very unusual woman by all accounts. Many dearly loved her, and her legacy evidently reaches far beyond her all-too-brief time in Helena. Clara was born on an Iowa farm in 1870. At the age of six, her family moved to the community of Humboldt, Iowa, founded by the Reverend S. H. Taft. This idealistic community shaped and inspired young Clara, who grew up under the guidance of Reverend Mary Safford of the Unity Unitarian Church, and public school principal Eleanor Gordon. After two years' training in Des Moines, Clara returned to Humboldt to teach kindergarten, a position she retained for eight years.

Reverend Safford accepted a new position, and thirty-year-old Edwin Stanton Hodgin arrived on the scene in 1898 as the new Unitarian minister. He was immediately smitten with Clara. She was uncertain, however, and after a lengthy courtship, she married the young minister on November 12, 1901. Two years later in 1903, the husband and wife were summoned as a team to Helena where Reverend Hodgin became the fifth pastor of the First Unitarian Church. The Hodgins quickly settled into their new community, relishing the beauty of Montana's landscape. The congregation was at that time struggling to pay for its

Clara Bicknell Hodgin. In Memoriam (Humboldt, Iowa, 1907).

magnificent new church. Within eighteen months the Hodgins had reduced the church's $8,000 debt to $4,500 and secured pledges for the remaining amount. By the end of 1904, Clara had endeared herself to the Unitarian congregation and the Helena community as well. Sunday school enrollment had increased from forty to over one hundred, and even non-members, including the superintendent of Helena's public schools, sought Clara's encouragement and advice.

The Unitarians believed that churches should serve the community, and so the building was designed by C.S. Haire to function as an auditorium/theater as well as a church. It was the perfect vehicle to combine Clara's creativity with her great love for children. Although the Hodgins had no children of their own, Clara took great delight in other people's sons and daughters. As superintendent of the Sunday school program, she directed her small charges in many dramatic presentations and appeared indefatigable.

Sadly, Clara began to suffer unusual bouts of insomnia and fatigue that worsened in November 1904. When her husband returned from a speaking engagement in Butte on December 4, he was alarmed to find his wife unable to get out of bed. Despite hospitalization, she continued to plan Christmas activities and characteristically laughed off her discomfort, giving friends the impression that she was healthier than she really was. Less that a month later, on January 14, 1905, Clara died at the age of thirty-four. An autopsy revealed a malignant abdominal tumor. A Methodist minister and a Jewish rabbi—as a tribute to her non-denominational friendships—conducted a quiet service that same evening at the Hodgins' home. In accordance with her wishes, her ashes were sent home to Humboldt where they were scattered into the Des Moines River. After a year, Reverend Hodgin moved to St. Paul, Minnesota.

Reverend Hodgin and Clara's parents received scores of letters from all over the country recalling and celebrating her life. Her family published some of them along with a short biography entitled *In Memoriam*, and sent a copy to the Helena Public Library in 1907. In spite of the flowery and sometimes maudlin turn-of-the-century sentiment, a portrait emerges of a remarkable woman who "loved her friends almost too fiercely," was idealistic almost to a fault, vivacious, full of humor, and deeply compassionate. Her grieving family marveled at what she left behind: "scores of notebooks filled with isolated thoughts and elaborate plans and outlines for future undertakings, hundreds of cards carefully arranged... and thousands of clippings carefully annotated and systematized. . . ." As a teacher, her classroom was known as the sunshine room: "If she were there the room was always full of sunshine, no matter what the weather." Reverend Duren Ward of Fort Collins, Colorado, praised her character as "rarely rounded, strong and beautiful." Eleven-year-old Selwyn Sharp, a former Des Moines kindergarten student, wrote, "There is one thing I can remember better than the games. That was her smile. I can remember it better than anything else."

Nor did Clara's Helena friends forget her. They established a memorial fund in her name and collected five hundred dollars—a substantial sum. Mrs. Harry Child commissioned renowned stained glass artist Louis Comfort Tiffany to craft in Clara's honor a small, exquisite memorial window reminiscent of a mountain sunset as seen from the Helena valley. It was installed in the church in 1907.

In 1933, the Unitarians donated their church to the City of Helena, and the building became the new home of the Lewis and Clark Public Library. The window was taken down, put away, and forgotten. After more than four decades as the public library, the grand old building was again renovated in 1976 to become the present Grandstreet Theatre. The theater had yet to open when Helena antique dealer Paul Martin happened across a listing of Tiffany windows made before 1910. The list also indicated where each had been shipped. Martin was astonished to learn of the window commissioned by Mrs. Child for Helena's Unitarian Church.

With the help of some senior citizens and a Civic Center custodian, Martin finally located the window hidden away in a basement corner. On December 6, 1976, one month after the first Grandstreet Theatre production, the window was returned to its original home under the delighted supervision of Eugene Sanden, Margaret Hibbard, and Katherine Towle. The three, who generously donated the substantial installation costs, had

attended Sunday school at the church and the window brought
back many childhood memories.

Typical of Tiffany windows of the period, when viewed
with no back lighting, it appears a marbled blue. Its appearance
changes dramatically with each subtle change in lighting. The
dedication at the bottom, "In Loving Memory of Clara Bicknell
Hodgin, 1905," sometimes becomes illegible while the upper window remains perfectly clear. The words look as if a childish hand
has smudged the paint on the glass. At other times, parts of the
window seem to have their own interior luminescence.

There is no question that extraordinary energy is at work in
the theater. Stage manager Debbye Gilleran recalled a troubling
incident after locking up following a performance. When she got
outside, Debbye was certain she had turned all the lights off, but
noticed one still burning in the women's restroom. She went back
in through the front door and hurried downstairs. She found
that more than one light had been either left on or turned back
on. She went back upstairs to check the house and stage. As she
entered the house from the stage end, she saw a white light that
looked like a shadow or a white mist on the north balcony stairs:
"It was an odd glow that shouldn't have been there." A check the
following night for possible reflections from passing cars or other
causes turned up no explanation.

Power tools and equipment turn on by themselves, lighting
sometimes malfunctions for no apparent reason, and items frequently
disappear. Theater school director Marianne Adams once searched
high and low for a two-year-old's missing sweater. She finally found
it folded neat as a pin in the child's toy pack. But everyone she asked
denied putting it there. Other incidents, however, are downright
creepy. Some have heard a man's laughter reverberate throughout
the empty building at night. During a performance of *Blithe Spirit*,
a theater patron seated at the back of the balcony next to a semi-

circular curtained window became very frightened. The window, originally designed to admit light into the church sanctuary, is high above the entry and inaccessible from the street. The patron noticed a ghastly face staring at him from outside the window. It continued to watch him throughout the production.

During a late-night rehearsal, one young teen had a scary encounter in the women's restroom. She was locked in a stall and heard the outer door open. Someone came in. As she was about to open the stall door, she heard a man whistling just on the other side. She looked underneath the stall door, but no one was there. When the whistling stopped she unlocked the door. The room was empty, but the outer door was swinging as if someone had just gone out.

Some of these encounters surely do not emanate from Clara. But whatever sinister spirits might lurk in the shadows at Grandstreet, Clara's positive energy keeps them from serious mischief. She hovers in the balcony watching and protecting. This intense, passionate woman left so many things undone and loved life so much that she can't bear to leave. Clara, who always seemed to bring sunshine with her, helps make Grandstreet and its theater school such a great success.

Helen Field Fischer, a Helena teacher, wrote a poem included on the title page of Clara's memorial. It might be interpreted as a promise of her lasting presence. Certainly it describes the legacy she left to all the aspiring players at today's Grandstreet Theatre. In part it reads:

> *She loved her life into a thousand lives.*
> *She cannot die, for when these lives awake*
> *And know that nevermore along Earth's ways*
> *Will pass that eager step and helping hand,*
> *A thousand lives will rise to consummate*
> *The purposes her flesh had failed to reach.* ❈

The Right Time

AMONG THE LAVISH, EXPENSIVE HOMES ON HELENA's West Side
is one stately mansion that commands a prominent place among
its Victorian-era neighbors. The home, now owned by Edwin T.
(Ted) Murphy, Jr. and Dorothy J. Fialho, is unusual and distinctive for its Tudor style, a rarity in Helena, with dark timbering
against pale stuccoed walls. Gothic-style arched windows soften
its handsome façade and beautiful stonework lends Old World
elegance. The stone of the foundation appears not to have been
custom-prepared for this home, suggesting that it was salvaged
from some other use. Jim Schulz, an expert on local stone quarries, says of all the many Helena buildings and residences that
he has studied, this particular home is the only one for which he
could not document a construction date, nor could he identify the
source of the stone. The home most likely dates to circa 1893.

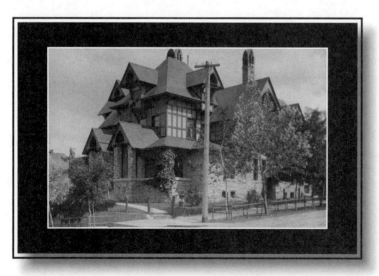

B. H. Tatem Residence, circa 1900. Montana Historical Society Photograph
Archives, Helena.

Helena's wealthy citizens who built their homes in the Upper West Side neighborhoods amassed fortunes in mining, cattle, banking, and real estate. Territorial Governor Samuel Hauser, U.S. Senator T.C. Power, mining magnate Thomas Cruse, legendary cattleman Conrad Kohrs, and many other wealthy Montanans kept West Side mansions in Montana's capital city. Benjamin H. Tatem, the original owner of this particular residence, held the position of U.S. Assayer at the federal assay office which still stands at 214 Broadway. This job was considered a real plum, obtained by presidential appointment. Tatem, who came to Helena in the early 1870s to manage the Unionville claims of the Philadelphia-owned Columbia Mining Company, operated one of Helena's first iron foundries on West Main Street and made substantial profits in gold mining at Marysville. President James McKinley appointed Tatem to the coveted position in 1901.

The prominent community-minded man died in 1915. In 1922, his eighty-two-year-old widow was enjoying fine health after a long recovery from a near-fatal accident. Several years previous she had been run over by a team of horses and severely injured. On the afternoon of January 24, 1922, the eastbound trolley at Lawrence Street and Benton Avenue fatally struck her as she crossed the street. An inquest found her death accidental, and the town mourned the passing of this well-known pioneer.

Neighbors remembered the Helena matron as one of the town's most hospitable and gracious hostesses. However, those who knew her well also remembered her intense paranoia of being robbed, and after entertaining had a habit of hiding her best silver in secret cubbyholes under the grand staircase. Later residents say that they would occasionally come across pieces of silverware tucked away in odd places and long forgotten. Evidence of the many parties guests enjoyed apparently still lingers in the spacious home which has stood vacant more often than it has been occupied in recent years. Residents say that they have occasionally seen a ghostly maid on her hands and knees scrubbing hardwood floors. More often, voices and music have been heard coming from the upper floor when no one else is there.

Spectral sounds are not that unusual in old houses, especially in Helena. There are other homes, such as the T.C. Power mansion, where this kind of ghostly partying is taken for granted. But the following event likely has less to do with the house than it has to do with the daughter of a recent resident. This family settled into the rambling mansion where the young girl had a nice room to herself, big enough to hold an extensive collection of dolls. The little girl spent hours arranging them just so. She soon began to notice that when she came home from school, her dolls were in different places and positions. She complained about it at first, accusing other family members of moving them around. No one would confess, and after a while she came to accept, even anticipate, the tampering.

One night she woke from a sound sleep. Standing next to her bed she saw what she thought was herself. She thought it was odd, like looking at her reflection where there wasn't a mirror. The child stared at her image, and the image stared back. She felt peculiarly drawn to this other self standing next to her. As the little girl fully awakened, the image vanished. The next morning the child was pensive over what she had seen, but kept it to herself fearing that her family would tease her.

Some time later the visitation reoccurred. This time the child was truly frightened and she decided to confide in her mother. Her mother asked her why she was so afraid. The child replied, with an insight way beyond her years, that it was not the image that was frightening, but rather her reaction to it. She sensed this "other self" was calling her, beckoning her, and she in turn felt connected to it. She feared that this was perhaps a foreboding prophecy, with her visitor signifying an untimely death. Her mother nodded with surprising empathy. The youngster fretted that her mother would make light of the experience and tell her it was just a dream. Instead, her mother offered this explanation: "You say that this image looked just like you? You know how you complain about someone moving your dolls around? Well, perhaps this might explain both things. Sometimes we really do have guardian angels watching over us. You are drawn to this look-alike because of a special connection you feel for each other. I have never told you about this because I believed that I would know when the time was right to share it. Now is the time. When you were born your father and I had reason to rejoice and grieve at the same time. I believe that what you have seen is your sister, your twin sister, who died when you were born." ✳

Montana Club's Urban Legend

> We waltzed our partners to the bar and treated them most free,
> Till guns would crack and lights go out with the utmost liberty.
> And when the sunlight touched the hills and flushed the circling
>   range
> The hangman's tree would loaded be with ghastly fruit and strange.
> For the old days were the great days,
> and Helena was the hub—
> Twas a Merry dance in old Last Chance
> and the Old Montana Club.
>
> Martin Maginnis, 1903

TALES OF GAMBLING, FREE-FLOWING LIQUOR, AND CAROUSING add to the mystique of Helena's elegant Montana Club. The club traces its long history back to an era when political and business decisions took place in the elegant back rooms of private clubs. Men instrumental in writing the state's history were its first members. Merchant prince T.C. Power, financier and politician Samuel Hauser, miner Thomas Cruse, copper kings William Clark, Marcus Daly, and Augustus Heinze, and businessman Anton Holter are a few. Legend has it that at various times members were all Republican, all Democrat, all Masons, all attorneys, or all millionaires. Though not true, there have been a number of members in each category.

Helena was at the threshold of its coming of age in the 1880s. The arrival of the Northern Pacific put this thriving territorial capital on the map in 1883. Wealthy residents with fortunes built upon mining, stock-raising, merchandising, and freighting worked hard to secure statehood and to promote Helena as the

"Queen City of the Rockies." To celebrate and promote this economic success, a group of young men met in the law office of E.W. Toole to found a social organization that would become tightly woven into Helena's, and Montana's, historic tapestry. Enrichment, not riches; elegance, not ostentation; and the good of the community were their goals. The Montana Club was destined to become an ambassador for the State of Montana and its capital city. In a very real sense, as historian Dave Walter points out, it is *Montana's* club, famed throughout the Pacific Northwest and well known across the nation as an elegant retreat. Today as yesterday, it is a pleasure to enter the club's sanctuary, where the visitor is shut away from the noise and bustle of a far more hectic world.

One historic event carefully detailed in the news of the day occurred on a cold night in April 1903. Fourteen-year-old Harry Anderson stealthily rode the elevator up to the sixth floor and deliberately set a fire. It was not the first time, nor even the second time, that young Harry, whose father was bartender at the club, had set fires. He loved to hear the alarm, watch the horse-drawn fire engine race to the fire, and observe the firemen as they worked the horses and equipment—they even let Harry help. But this night, the wind whipped through Last Chance Gulch, fanning the flames into the club's upper floors. There was neither a ladder tall enough nor water pressure powerful enough to reach the top stories. The fire consumed the impressive landmark floor by floor. By dawn only the stone arches stood among the charred and smoldering remains. Harry was swiftly sentenced to the boys' reform school at Miles City, but was defended gratis by club member Thomas Walsh, later a U.S. senator. There at Pine Hills School for Boys, young Harry spent the remainder of his youth.

The second Montana Club, rebuilt incorporating the original ground-floor arches, literally rose from the ashes of the first

The Montana Club at Sixth and Fuller Avenues. L. H. Jorud, photographer (July 11, 1931). Montana Historical Society Archives, Helena.

building and resumed its role in hosting politicians, millionaires, and even presidents within its lofty halls and elegant rooms. They enjoyed drinks at its bar, mixed and served by Julian Anderson, young Harry's father. Because Julian was so beloved by the community and so loyal to his patrons, Harry's misdeeds were rarely discussed. Julian's unusual story began with his birth in Germany to slaves whose wealthy southern owners had fled there to escape the Civil War. He returned to the United States at the age of five. When he was old enough to make his own way, he came west and ended up in Helena. Anderson claimed never to have taken a drink himself, but began tending bar at the Montana Club in 1893 and retired sixty years later in 1953. Even during Prohibition, Anderson remained at the bar, mixing drinks from members' private reserves stored in lockers in the basement.

Visitors were suitably impressed by the amenities offered at the Montana Club and thereby suitably impressed with Helena. Club steward Edmund O'Connell loved to relate how, during the 1890s, one local member invited some Easterners to Helena in the hope of securing financial backing for large-scale mining operations that required large capital investments. Members whisked the guests from the train depot to the Montana Club where they received royal treatment. When the club closed at 2 AM, guests were conveyed to the "Castle" where a bevy of ladies, under the tutelage of madam Lillie Ashton, entertained them until dawn. The visitors then boarded the train for their return to the East. Once back home, an acquaintance asked one of the visitors where he had been. "Helena, Montana," he replied. "How big a place is that?" asked the acquaintance. Thinking back upon his whirl-wind adventure in the Queen City, and estimating the population which then actually stood at about thirteen thousand, the traveler replied, "Judging from what I saw, I'd say half a million."

Through women's suffrage the club survived, softening its rules to include escorted women on certain days and at certain times. The Great Depression took its toll on membership, but with Prohibition over, the bar "officially" reopened in 1934. Restrictions on women eased and in spite of anti-gambling legislation, "one-armed bandits" reportedly brought new prosperity to the club. Legalized in private clubs by the start of World War II, the slot machines whirred in the basement Rathskeller and the second-floor lounge. Women reportedly lined up outside the door at nine in the morning waiting to play the slots, and the club employed seven bartenders and three barmaids to serve the crowds.

Club lore includes scores of political deals made, fortunes won and lost, and scandals. The cavernous building with its rich ornamental woods and spacious hallways offered comparatively Spartan accommodations for single men, but during the 1920s and on into the Depression, families lived on its residential floors. The six levels today include modernized offices, a club dining room, kitchen, several smaller dining rooms, a lounge, and the basement Rathskeller, which occasionally hosts private parties. In the midst of one of the middle floors, there is a turn-of-the-century smoking room in pristine condition. Beautifully paneled walls, coffered ceilings, built-in bookcases, and humidor cabinets with doors of yellow bottle glass epitomize what one might imagine a men's smoking room ought to look like. The grandeur of the elegant Montana Club is evident throughout the building. The club also has its secrets.

Manager J. Anne Roberts, a most gracious hostess, related an incident that followed a wedding reception at the club. Just after midnight, she and two employees were cleaning the dining room. The club was quiet and they looked forward to the end of a long evening. The sound of the phone ringing in the dark, silent club made them jump. J. Anne answered, and the voice on the other end identified himself as a Helena police officer. "Is everything okay there?" J. Anne was puzzled at the question and answered that, as far as she knew, everything was in order.

The officer informed her that the 911 operator had received several emergency calls. The telephone number identification indicated that the calls had been made from inside the Montana Club. J. Anne was astonished at this, assuring the officer that only the three of them were in the building and none of them had made calls that evening. Nevertheless, he dispatched officers to make a floor-by-floor check. It was nearly 2 AM before they had finished. The officers went out shaking their heads. "We didn't find anything," they reported, "but this building is so vast, and there are so many rooms, that we can't guarantee the building is empty. Someone could even be living here and no one would know. This place is a crime scene waiting for a crime." The mysterious caller was never found. ✸

Epilogue

Several years ago I was lucky enough to have been recruited to help research the Montana Club's history and script a tour for visitors. Manager J. Anne Roberts allowed me free access to the many rooms and answered my questions. The two of us had a connection: in 1988 we had purchased our home from her husband, Joe. On occasion J. Anne and I had discussed the incidents in my house. I asked her about ghosts at the Montana Club. She just raised an eyebrow and mentioned that employees refused to go into the basement at night. She didn't elaborate, but made it clear that they had their reasons. Bartender Ken Jacques confirmed that the employees were definitely wary of the basement after dark.

One afternoon J. Anne, a colleague of mine, and I were standing in the hallway between the two private dining rooms on the Mezzanine. The central hall at that time had several glass display cases filled with antiques related to the club. One piece was a heavy Art Deco vase in the shape of a woman's head. The face formed the bottom, and the woman's hair fanned out above creating a wide opening at the top. Her billowing hair appeared as if it were under water. We were discussing the unusual appearance of this particular piece, and not in very complimentary terms. The door to the President's Room was at my left elbow, propped open with a doorstop. Unexpectedly, the heavy paneled door slammed shut with such ferocity that it rattled the china in the display cases. J. Anne observed that someone didn't appreciate our comments, and went on to say that slamming doors were commonplace.

On another occasion, J. Anne and I discussed the tales that abound in Helena and many western towns of underground tunnels. This was a thread that I needed to address in scripting a tour of the building. Many Helenans firmly believe that Chinese residents had a system of underground opium dens that criss-crossed beneath much of the town. They further maintain that another system of tunnels in downtown Helena connected houses of ill repute with respectable businesses. There is no evidence to substantiate these stories in Helena. There was, however, an underground heating system linking downtown businesses to a central steam heating plant. The Montana Club had such a passageway, but seems not to have tapped into the city's system, the club having always been equipped with its own boiler.

J. Anne gave us a tour of the basement, reiterating the fact that employees refuse to roam the halls down there after dark. She let us wander in the bar called the Rathskeller, and admire its dark stained wood, faux leather walls, and corner fireplace. She showed us the lockers where Julian Anderson kept members' private liquor reserves during Prohibition and the Rathskeller's outer edges where murky light filters through the glass ceiling blocks that pave the street-level sidewalk above. J. Anne led my colleague and me through a maze of corridors to the boiler room. She wanted us to see the padlocked doorway to the city's old central heating plant. Such places are always creepy, but this area of the old club with its huge boiler and heavy, locked door was eerily reminiscent of Stephen King's haunted hotel boiler room in *The Shining*. As we stood there speculating on the mythical use of Helena's tunnels, I noticed something glinting at the juncture of the floor and wall near the tunnel door. Half concealed in the sandy debris that crumbled from the old foundation was a red cat's eye marble, *spirit tailings* of the old Montana Club. ❂

Sources

Axline, Jon., et al. *More From The Quarries of Last Chance Gulch.* Vols I–III. Helena, MT: American & World Publishing, 1994, 1996, 1998.

Baumler, Ellen. "Devil's Perch: Prostitution from Suite to Cellar in Butte, Montana." *Montana The Magazine of Western History* 48 (1998): 4–21.

Baumler, Ellen. "More than the Glory: Preserving the Gold Rush and Its Outcome at Virginia City." *Montana The Magazine of Western History* 49 (1999): 64–75.

Gilmore, Sister Julia, S.C.L. *We Came North: The Centennial Story of the Sisters of Charity of Leavenworth.* St. Meinrad, IN: Abbey Press, 1958.

Howard, Joseph Kinsey. *Montana High Wide and Handsome.* New Haven: Yale University, 1943.

Hutchens, John K. *One Man's Montana: An Informal Portrait of a State.* Philadelphia: Lippincott, 1964.

Malone, Michael, Richard B. Roeder and William L. Lang. *Montana: A History of Two Centuries.* rev. ed. Seattle: University of Washington, 1995.

Merriam, H.G., ed. *Frontier Woman: The Memoirs of Mary Ronan as told to Margaret Ronan.* Missoula, MT: University of Montana, 1973.

Munn, Debra D. *Big Sky Ghosts: Eerie True Tales of Montana.* Vols 1 & 2. Boulder, CO: Pruett, 1993 & 1994.

Pace, Dick. *Golden Gulch: The Story of Montana's Fabulous Alder Gulch.* East Wenatchee, WA: Jursnick, 1962.

Paladin, Vivian and Jean Baucus. *Helena: An Illustrated History.* Helena, MT: Montana Historical Society Press, 1983.

Petrik, Paula. *No Step Backward.* Helena, MT: Montana Historical Society Press, 1987.

Towle, Virginia Rose. *Vigilante Woman.* New York: A.S. Barnes, 1966.

Wolle, Muriel Sibell. *Montana Pay Dirt: A Guide to the Mining Camps of the Treasure State.* Denver: Sage Books, 1963.

Writer's Program, WPA. *Copper Camp: Stories of the World's Greatest Mining Town, Butte, Montana.* New York: Hastings, 1943.

Spirit Tailings Index